Also of Interest

Renewable Energy Resources and Rural Applications in the Developing World, edited by Norman L. Brown

Water in a Developing World: The Management of a Critical Resource, edited by Albert E. Utton and Ludwik A. Teclaff

*Managing Development in the Third World, Coralie Bryant and Louise G. White

*Renewable Natural Resources: A Management Handbook for the Eighties, edited by Dennis L. Little, Robert E. Dils, and John Gray

*The Economics of Environmental and Natural Resources Policy, edited by J. A. Butlin

Managing Ocean Resources: A Primer, edited by Robert L. Friedheim

*Food from the Sea: The Economics and Politics of Ocean Fisheries, Frederick W. Bell

Aquaculture Development in Less Developed Countries: Social, Economic, and Political Problems, edited by Leah J. Smith and Susan Peterson

Aquaculture Economics: Basic Concepts and Methods of Analysis, Yung C. Shang

Successful Seed Programs: A Planning and Management Guide, edited by Johnson E. Douglas

Small Farm Development: Understanding and Improving Farming Systems in the Humid Tropics, Richard R. Harwood

Water Needs for the Future: Political, Economic, Legal, and Technological Issues in a National and International Framework, edited by Ved P. Nanda

*From Dependency to Development: Strategies to Overcome Underdevelopment and Inequality, edited by Heraldo Muñoz

Energy From Biological Processes, Office of Technology Assessment, U.S. Congress

*Available in hardcover and paperback.

Managing Renewable
Natural Resources
in Developing Countries

Westview Special Studies in Social, Political, and Economic Development

Managing Renewable Natural Resources in Developing Countries
edited by Charles W. Howe

Much of the improvement in material living standards in the Third World is attributable to the exploitation of nonrenewable resources such as fossil fuels and metallic ores, and to the exploitation of renewable resource systems at rates that cannot be sustained. This state of affairs presents a serious problem for the future; just as may be the case for the developed regions, a long-term perspective shows clearly that Third World countries must return to a greater dependence on renewable resources while also avoiding irreversible degradation of renewable systems and learning to manage these systems more productively.

The authors of this book examine major issues in the four main renewable resource sectors--fisheries, forestry, agriculture, and water--with emphasis on the problems and benefits attendant to various use patterns and management practices.

Dr. Charles W. Howe is professor of economics at the University of Colorado. He has been a visiting professor of economics at the University of Nairobi, Kenya, and director of the Water Resources Program for Resources for the Future, Inc., a Washington, D.C., research institute. He is author of Natural Resources Economics: Issues, Analysis, and Policy.

Managing Renewable Natural Resources in Developing Countries

edited by Charles W. Howe

Contributors

H. Stuart Burness
Marion Clawson
James A. Crutchfield
Ronald G. Cummings
Charles W. Howe
D. Gale Johnson
Roger A. Sedjo

Westview Press / Boulder, Colorado

Westview Special Studies in Social, Political, and Economic Development

Copyright © 1982 by Westview Press, Inc.

Published in 1982 in the United States of America by
    Westview Press, Inc.
    5500 Central Avenue
    Boulder, Colorado 80301
    Frederick A. Praeger, President and Publisher

Library of Congress Cataloging in Publication Data
Main entry under title:
Managing renewable natural resources in developing countries.
    (Westview special studies in social, political, and economic development)
    Includes index.
    1. Underdeveloped areas--Natural resources--Management. I. Howe,
Charles W. II. Series.
HC59.7.M2593   333.7'09172'4   82-2055
ISBN 0-86531-313-X   AACR2

Composition for this book was provided by the editor
Printed and bound in the United States of America

Contents

Tables

Figures

Preface

The chapters of this book were originally given in a sequence of workshops in The Seminar on the Economics of Renewable Natural Resources sponsored by the Ministry of Agriculture and Fundación Chile in Santiago, Chile in December, 1980. The papers were so complementary, addressing an interlocked set of issues at the heart of development planning these days, that it seemed appropriate to expand them with the benefit of the seminar discussions and to publish them as a unit. The authors wish to thank the sponsoring agencies for the opportunity of working together in a stimulating environment, while emphasizing that the opinions expressed are those of the authors alone.

Charles W. Howe is Professor of Natural Resource Economics at the University of Colorado - Boulder. James A. Crutchfield is Professor of Economics at the University of Washington - Seattle. Marion Clawson is Consultant in Residence and Roger A. Sedjo is Director of the Forest Economics and Policy Program at Resources for the Future, Inc., Washington, D.C. D. Gale Johnson is Professor and Chairman of the Department of Economics, University of Chicago. Ronald G. Cummings and H. Stuart Burness are Professors of Economics at the University of New Mexico - Albuquerque.

Charles W. Howe

Managing Renewable
Natural Resources
in Developing Countries

1
A Challenge
to the Developing Countries

Charles W. Howe

There is increasing concern within international organizations and national governments about the adequacy
of the natural resource bases of the developing countries.
Much of the observed improvement in material living standards in the Third World is attributable to the exploitation of non-renewable resources like the fossil fuels and
metallic ores <u>or</u> to non-sustainable rates of exploitation
of renewable resource systems such as forestry, fisheries,
agriculture, and related water systems. In the longer
term, the developing countries must <u>return</u> to a greater
dependence on renewable resources. This is a long term
process of avoiding non-reversible degradation of renewable systems, of investing wisely, and learning to manage
the systems more productively.

Irreversible changes in renewable resource systems
always pose difficult questions for the decision-maker.
Shall we build a reservoir with its near term useful outputs of water, power, flood control, and fisheries, knowing that the valley being taken out of production can
never be returned to other uses? Shall the native forests be cleared of their highly valued timber, knowing
that the natural forest can never be regrown? Should
fish stocks that offer a valuable protein source be reduced to levels at which the probability of extinction is
significant? Should mono-cultures of specialized crop
varieties be promoted, knowing that many local varieties
that have been adapted to a particular niche will be lost
and not available for future adaptive breeding?

In fisheries, the avoidance of irreversibilities involves not only maintenance of viable fish stocks through
control of fishing effort, but the protection of water
quality to an extent that fisheries are not endangered by
toxic materials and anaerobic conditions. Many of the most
valuable and unique fisheries including lobster, prawns,
and shrimp have been lost to massive amounts of very

1

simple, degradable, easily treated organic wastes.

In forestry, the rapid progress of deforestation is causing worldwide concern, especially regarding tropical zones. Highland rainforests that are crucial as watersheds and to the generation of soil are rapidly and non-selectively being denuded. The three great regions of lowland tropical rainforest, the Amazon, West and Central Africa, and Southeast Asia, are all experiencing rapid deforestation, usually not by chance but as a matter of policy. The extrapolation of present trends to the end of this century indicates the practical elimination of lowland tropical rainforest.

In agriculture, the avoidance of irreversible changes involves the avoidance of highly erodible soils, the use of proper drainage in irrigated areas, the controlled use of brackish waters for irrigation, sustaining soil texture and chemistry, the avoidance of chemical build-ups in soils and water bodies, and informed limitations on the introduction of mono-cultures.

In the water sector, water sources must be protected against destruction of both their quantity and quality. These considerations tie water resources directly to all other sectors of the economy, including the other renewable resource sectors. Forests provide natural watersheds. Agriculture consumes enormous quantities of water and, through its return flows, affects water quality. Fishery viability may not be compatible with the damming of streams or the overuse of streams as waste conduits. Land uses of all types contribute to erosion, the resulting sediments of which will fill all our reservoirs in the next century. How dependent should we become on those reservoirs?

In each of these cases, the steps required to avoid irreversible changes have large, near-term costs associated with them: lower fish catches, smaller opportunities to transform natural forest capital into currently scarcer forms of man-made capital. For lower income regions of the world, the trade-off of immediate benefits for long-term sustainability of the system is a cruel choice that indicates the great need for rational, objective decision-making about the management, further development, or depletion of these systems.

Some regions of the developing world are fortunate enough to have both valuable non-renewable resources and still viable renewable resource systems. The absence of either severely limits future possibilities. The proceeds from petroleum, gas, some minerals, and the reduction of valuable forest inventories provide streams of capital that can be reinvested in the renewable resource sectors, in exploration for further stocks of non-renewables, and in research that will increase the productivity of those sectors. The reinvestment of this capital in carefully selected, high-return, long-lived economic activities is crucial to the long term viability of these countries.

The chapters of this book treat some of the main issues of the four major renewable resource systems: fisheries, forestry, agriculture, and water. Emphasis is placed on problems created by externalities from renewable resource use or from the modes of management being used. Examples include the negative effects of free entry into fisheries, the positive externalities of agricultural research knowledge, the watershed benefits or disbenefits of forest management practices, and the interdependencies of water uses on a common water body.

A bioeconomic approach to fisheries management emphasizes the need to deal with vast uncertainties about the fish stock and the problem of free entry of harvesting resources into the fishery. The distributional and cultural effects that are likely to occur as a result of moving from traditional fishing systems to more viable and efficient systems are given particular emphasis.

Agricultural concerns center on agricultural research. Smaller developing countries cannot support pioneering basic research, but they have many opportunities and, indeed, the necessity of engaging in adaptive research. While information is transferable from the larger temperate zone countries and the international research centers, it always requires adaptation. A significant level of agricultural research and extension activity are necessary simply to maintain current levels of productivity against the incursion of diseases and pests. Rates of return from all such research are known to be high. Some questions addressed are, "How much should be invested in agricultural research?" "What institutional settings should be used?" "What is the role of the private sector and of competition among research centers?"

Forestry is analyzed in terms of the world-wide distribution of mature forest cover and the climatic advantages of the sub-tropics for forestry. It is demonstrated that the sub-tropical Third World countries have an increasingly strong comparative advantage for forestry. Alternative management policies are treated in terms of their effects on other sectors, on land use, and on employment.

The issues raised about water development and management relate primarily to the institutional framework within which these activities take place, especially the roles of the public and private sectors. Water systems are unique in the degree of interdependence of the users of the system. Upstream-downstream, groundwater-surface water, and water quality relationships all serve to bind users together through a network of what economists call "externalities," i.e. physical interdependencies that aren't included in market transactions. This makes the evaluation of benefits and costs difficult, but it tremendously increases the complexity of the reallocation of water over time--a vital function in the face of high costs or nonavailability of new water supplies.

Various systems for establishing property rights and markets in water are compared. The meaning and various roles of the "pricing" of water are investigated and related both to the financial management and economic efficiency characteristics of water systems. Possible roles for and complications from large interbasin transfers of water are discussed.

The institutional framework generally evolves from a complex variety of pressures representing the various objectives and groups that are served by water development. While it is difficult to make any general prescriptions about this framework, it is certainly possible for countries to learn from the long history of institutional development in other countries. Thus, the final chapter analyzes the changes in underlying policy and the practical manifestations of these changes in the history of United States' water development. The very subtle changes are traced from early attempts to impose "market-like" tests of the viability of public irrigation projects to recognition that irrigated agriculture is unlikely to be able to "pay its own way" directly and that water development serves numerous objectives other than irrigation.

The countries of the Third World that are seeking rapid economic and social development today face quite different situations regarding their renewable natural resources than did the countries that developed rapidly during the 19th century. Today's developing countries have available technologies and large international markets that make massive exploitation of renewable resource systems both possible and temptingly attractive. At the same time, population densities and limited geographical frontiers don't give them the room to make big mistakes with their renewable systems. In the United States' context, the creation of a dustbowl, the depletion of the soil, or the non-renewed cutting of a vast region's timber meant that people had to move on to the next frontier, at least until their systems gradually renewed themselves. Today's developing countries don't have these options. They must do a more deliberate job of managing their renewable resources.

2
The Economics
of Fisheries Management

James A. Crutchfield

INTRODUCTION

In this paper I propose to discuss the state of the
art of fisheries management from the vantage point of a
natural resource economist. Our view of man's impact on
exploited marine fish stocks has gone through an evolu-
tionary process, running from the naive concept of open
fisheries in oceans of inexhaustible fertility, through
the concept of maximum sustained physical yield, to more
sophisticated multiobjective programs in which physical
productivity of stocks, economic efficiency, equity in
the distribution of jobs and incomes, and social stabil-
ity and improvement all play a role. Unfortunately,
many fishery managers are still hard aground in one of
the earlier stages. The sober tone of this paper reflects continuing frustration over man's apparent inabil-
ity to pursue rationally the full economic benefits that
living marine resources and the progress of fisheries
science have made available.

We begin by reviewing the factors that complicate
marine fisheries and make the problems of both harvester
and manager different in kind as well as degree from
those faced in the use of other natural resources. In
the second section, the objectives of fishery management
are discussed briefly, with emphasis on the need to
couple biological objectives to economic and social concerns. This is followed by a discussion of management
techniques. Attention is centered on the weaknesses of
management measures that ignore economic repercussions,
and on broader concepts of management programs that promise better protection of fish stocks while permitting
greater economic benefits.

The final section explores the implications of these
developments for developing countries, especially those
in the Southern Hemisphere, where many opportunities for
effective development of under-utilized fishery resources
are still to be found. Special emphasis is placed on the

information systems required to make fishery management worthwhile and on the inevitable constraints on the gains from management stemming from the incredibly complex environment in which marine resources are found.

COMPLICATIONS PECULIAR TO THE DEVELOPMENT AND MANAGEMENT OF FISHERY RESOURCES

Common Property

By long tradition, fishermen throughout the world regard the right to go fishing as one of fundamental, almost religious, significance, despite the overwhelming evidence that the right of everyone to go fishing freely inevitably results in the erosion of the value of such rights. While the destructiveness of competitive fishing under open access conditions is now almost universally recognized, the problems associated with conversion to a system of controlled property rights have proved to be extremely difficult. These will be explored in the following sections; suffice it to say at this point that no combination of fishery management techniques that fails to deal with the common property problem offers any real hope of economic benefit from management. In most cases, even the biological objective of protecting the productivity of the stocks involved cannot be achieved without limiting fishing effort.

Instability of Natural Systems

Fisheries are subject to wide variations in yields as a result of changes in the complex marine environment. These changes in yield-effort relations (and therefore in cost per unit of catch) may reflect changes in the total number of fish; their accessibility (i.e., concentration in schools and/or distance from shore); and catchability (i.e., under some conditions fish may be more difficult to catch even though numbers and concentrations are identical). As a result, commercial fishing has been aptly described as an industry always in a state of short-run disequilibrium. These changes in supply conditions, reflecting primarily very large changes in the size of spawning groups recruited successively to a commercial fishery,* make it extraordinarily difficult to plan fishing operations as a more conventional business operation would.

---

*Marine fish spawn at intervals, and the survivors of each group are said to be "recruited into the fishery" when they are large enough to be taken by commercial fishermen.

Data Problems

Finally, the inherent uncertainty about available supplies of fish and the resulting instability of operating costs for fishing ventures are accentuated by the difficulty and cost of developing reliable data. Marine fish populations cannot be viewed directly; the size and condition of commercially important stocks can only be estimated indirectly on the basis of catch, effort, and age/size sample data. But these can be obtained at acceptable cost only from the commercial fishery itself. As a result, the data required to assess and monitor marine fish populations are frequently incomplete (particularly with respect to the amount of effort expended and the location of fish catches), and are badly biased; fishermen do not fish in a random fashion, but seek out known or expected areas of concentration. Added to this is the generally suspect nature of data reported by fishermen around the world. Since these reports are linked, at least in the fisherman's mind, with potential tax liabilities or regulations of various types, there is a persistent tendency toward under reporting. Moreover, the proprietary importance to a successful fisherman of information about good fishing grounds, seasonal variations in availability, etc., means that such information is not readily disclosed, even to supposedly neutral management authorities. It is accurate rather than flippant to say that the all-important records of fish catches and effort, on which stock assessment and any kind of rational fishery management must rest, range from mediocre to nonexistent. And the cost of supplementing and verifying reported data from the commercial fishery by research vessels is prohibitive in all but a handful of cases.

It should also be pointed out that there are unfortunate and almost irreducible lags between the time fish are actually taken and the time the resulting reported data can be analyzed and converted into meaningful management recommendations; and between imposition of needed regulation and the realization of tangible benefits.

Space limitations preclude full exploration of a further complication, the multi-species fishery problem, but its importance calls for at least limited discussion. Most analysis of the biological and economic consequences of fishing and fishery management is limited to one or two species. Fish populations are linked, biologically, in enormously complex ways that defy accurate quantification at present. Many commercially important species stand in predator-prey relationships; heavy exploitation of the forage stocks may have serious repercussions on other populations which feed on them. In other cases, competition for common food sources or for space creates complex interactions among stocks. The one feature

8

common to all these interdependencies is their incredible complexity. To assume that selective harvesting of "target" populations leaves other related species completely unchanged can be dangerously misleading; yet our ability to explain the linkages and to quantify them is so severely limited that we often have no option but to ignore them.

Another aspect of the "multi-species problem" is technological. Many types of fishing gear will take several species simultaneously, with only limited ability to alter the composition of the catch (by changing mesh sizes, areas fished, or time of fishing, for example).

Finally, the typical fishing vessel can be deployed and/or equipped to harvest more than one stock as prices and availability of fish dictate. A full analysis of both biological and economic effects of fishing and of fishery management must take into account the range of alternatives available to the fleets involved.

The joint harvesting of several stocks, whatever the underlying reason, leads to two general conclusions. First, the physical yield from the complex related fish populations will be lower than the theoretical maximum that could be obtained if each stock could be harvested selectively. Second, concentration upon the "right" levels of catch for the most important species means that less productive stocks will be depleted (perhaps to the point of extinction) while more productive populations will be producing less than their full capability.

From a management standpoint, these biological and technological linkages among exploited fish stocks make an already complex set of decisions and data requirements even more burdensome. Yet they cannot be ignored entirely, and as man presses harder upon marine fish populations the economic importance of species interdependency becomes even greater.

A number of conclusions can be drawn from this somewhat sombre view of the basis for fishery management. First, determination of basic data requirements and establishment of the necessary data collection system are absolutely essential first steps in developing any kind of management regime. Second, we tend to expect too much of fishery management. The burdens placed on fishery scientists, statisticians, and decision makers are such that management of marine fisheries must always be an exercise in second or third best. Third, it is quite possible that for some fisheries the cost of collecting the necessary data and the framework of regulation and enforcement may exceed any benefits to be obtained. While the fishery may, as a result, tend toward excessive capitalization and perhaps some depletion, management would simply cost more than it is worth.

WHY MANAGE FISHERY RESOURCES?

The question is a legitimate one. Why shouldn't the
development and utilization of living marine resources be
carried on in a market-oriented economy by private individuals or firms, guided by competitive forces to time-
rates of use that are also satisfactory to society? One
answer to the question is empirical--wherever one looks,
mature fisheries show the same depressing pattern: a
flush period of rapid development and good profits, followed by a subsequent decline in productivity, very low
returns to all factors of production, and--too frequently
--physical depletion or even extinction of the resource
itself. The pattern seems to hold regardless of whether
the fishery is exploited by a single nation or by groups
of nations; and it proceeds to its remorseless and unpal-
atable conclusion most rapidly where prices of the end
products are high relative to harvesting costs.
The economic theory of an open access or common
property resource suggests analytic reasons why this general tendency toward unsatisfactory rates of use of living marine resources should be so nearly universal. The
yield that can be taken from a population of animals of
any kind is dependent on the rates at which new individuals are recruited to the exploitable population; growth
rates of the individuals; natural mortality rates, and
the rate of predation by man himself. In less formal
terms, the level of exploitation of a marine fishery
today has a significant influence on the size and aggregate weight of the fish that will be available for harvest in the future. Given reasonable estimates of the
biological functions mentioned above, the prices of fish
and the costs of labor and capital required, maximization
of economic benefit from the fishery would call for a
level of fishing effort that would maximize the present
value of the stream of benefits available over time. A
single owner of a fishery would rarely find it profitable
to "mine" the resource. Rather, he would make sure that
the productivity of the stock is maintained and that the
yield that can be safely taken, period by period, is
harvested at the lowest possible cost.
Under common property or open access conditions, the
vital link between the level of today's harvest and the
availability of fish in the future is hopelessly rup-
tured. No individual fisherman or group of fishermen can
control the current rate of harvesting if the fishery is
open to any new entrant. Even though he may be well
aware that by catching less today he will provide for
catches in the future enough larger to make it worth his
while to "invest in the stock," any curtailment of his
current catch simply results in an increase for someone
else. Even if all fishermen, actual and potential, were
well aware of the fact that additional fishing effort

would actually reduce the total catch, it would still pay
new entrants to build vessels and enter the race if
prices and costs make the potential return sufficiently
attractive.

Thus, both theory and a long series of industry
studies lead to the disheartening conclusion that unlim-
ited entry to a marine fishery will inevitably result in
excessive quantities of capital and labor, over-exploita-
tion of the resource, and, in the case of very attractive
fish stocks, biological depletion in varying degrees.
Unfortunately, the actual economic performance of a heavily exploited, open-access fishery is likely to be even
worse. In the real world, the availability of fish from
year to year is difficult, and in most cases impossible,
to predict with any accuracy. During the years of high
catches or high prices (or both), it is very easy to
bring new vessels into the fishery. During the inevitable periods of declining catches and/or low prices, however, fishermen will continue to operate their gear as
long as out-of-pocket expenses can be covered since there
is little or nothing one can do with a fishing vessel
except fish--and a shift to other fishing operations simply generalizes the problem of over-capacity.

Thus, the bursts of new entry during the good years
are rarely matched by exit from the industry when the
fishery is under either economic or biological pressure.
The result is a tendency toward chronic, dragging under-
employment, low incomes, and a variety of social ills
that accompany that combination. The problem is further
accentuated by the widespread tendency toward cultural
and economic immobility of low-income fishermen in scattered fishing communities.

I stress the fact that this sketch of economic
behavior in a fishery open to everyone is not a theoretical exercise; it is a disturbingly general description of
mature commercial fisheries worldwide. The matter is
muddled further by the nature of the costs to society of
excessive rates of use of common property fisheries under
open access. There may be a loss of potential yield in
fish, but there is certain to be a much greater loss of
other goods that could have been produced with the large
volumes of redundant capital and labor in the fishery
whose marginal value product is zero or negative. Over-
fishing in this economic sense will always exist in an
open fishery, even when fishermen's incomes are reasonably good and when the resource is in no danger of
depletion.

THE OBJECTIVES OF MANAGEMENT

With increasing concern over world protein shortages, society has a right to expect better use of living

resources of the sea. Economic analysis offers no in-
stant cures, but it does suggest unequivocally that the
root of the problem--the common property issue--must be
resolved before any lasting hope for improvement in economic and biological performance of commercial fisheries
can be expected.

While intervention of some kind is required to prevent an open access fishery from devouring itself, intervention to date has been remarkably unsuccessful in
achieving economic gains. The reason may well lie in
objectives. Virtually every management program concerned
with living marine resources has specified (or implied)
maximum sustained yield as its objective. Apart from the
statistical problems of defining exactly what this might
mean with respect to a particular fishery, it is not a
meaningful goal even in a biological sense; and it
becomes hopelessly inadequate if one views the fishery
as a means of improving human well being. Even in the
narrow sense of physical yield, the implicit assumptions
that stock-yield-fishing effort relationships are completely stable over time and that exploitation is
directed at single stocks violate what every fisherman
knows to be true. Maximizing the yield from a given fish
population leaves open the possibility that shifting
fishing effort to a larger or more accessible stock could
produce much larger catches. Put in this light, MSY
always breaks down to MSY of commercially valuable
species. But this simply means that the objective is
not really maximization of physical yield but an improp-
erly specified economic goal.

A broader and more useful set of objectives for
fishery management, couched in terms familiar to other
resource-oriented industries, would include the following:
1. Protection of the productivity of the stocks.
Regardless of any other concern for efficient use of the
resource, the endless uncertainty about the status of
marine fish populations requires that management authorities be able to take immediate and direct action to deal
with emergency situations (e.g., unexpected failures of
spawning classes or unusually heavy deployment of fishing
gear in a particular locality).
2. Flexibility. Given the high degree of uncertainty about the availability of fish, fishery management
must be able to respond flexibly to changing situations
during a fishing season as well as between seasons.
3. Correct level of catch. In formal terms, this
would be the level of catch at which the marginal social
value of the harvest is equated to the incremental social
costs required to take it (including management costs).
4. The right size (age) composition of catch. No
net economic gains can be realized by allowing fish to
grow larger before harvest; in formal terms, marginal

increments to revenue from growth in size of individual
fish are just offset by marginal losses to natural mortality.

   5. The right number and kind of fishing vessel/gear
combinations. Any given level of catch is taken at the
lowest possible cost, with optimal factor combinations in
each fishing unit and an optimal number of units.

   6. Optimal fleet deployment. Ideally fishing effort should be deployed geographically so that no increase in yield and/or reduction in costs can be achieved
by changing fishing areas or times.

   In short, the prime objective of fishery management
should be to maximize the present value of the fishing
operation, subject to rather severe constraints arising
from the instability of the target populations and the
cost and scantiness of timely data.

   As in all natural resource development and management programs, however, efficient use of the resource is
a necessary but not a sufficient condition for overall
social efficiency. We are concerned, for example, that
income and employment opportunities in the fisheries be
distributed in a reasonably equitable manner. If possible, we would choose a type of fishing program that
minimized fluctuations in employment and income. And
short-term requirements with respect to balance of payments might sometimes dictate different levels of exploitation than pure economic efficiency would suggest.

   As an aside, it might be noted that these noneffi-
ciency considerations in fishery management should be
viewed with a slightly suspicious eye. The temptation
to use commercial fishing industries as concealed unemployment schemes is very strong, and social considerations in fishery management are often no more than
cleverly concealed arguments for the status quo--and the
preservation of a simple, untroubled life for the admin-
istrator.

TRADITIONAL MANAGEMENT MEASURES

   Protection of the productivity of fish stocks can be
achieved, in theory, by any of a number of techniques
that reduce fishing mortality. These include time closures, area closures, restrictions on more efficient types
of vessels and gear, quotas, and restrictions on the
total amount of fishing inputs (that is, the labor and
capital actually employed). Traditionally, fishery
management has tended to emphasize the first four techniques. But again, both theory and experience suggest
strongly that attempts to control total catch by any
measure or combination of measures that still allow free
entry to the industry are doomed to failure. As indicated by a number of authors (see, for example,

Crutchfield, 1961; Scott, 1962; and Anderson, 1977) attempts to reduce catch by time or area closures are ineffective unless they raise fishermen's costs significantly. Thus, the operative control is not the closure itself but the effect of making the fish too expensive to catch.

Similarly, overall quota systems (for example, in the Pacific halibut and Southeast Pacific tuna fisheries) invariably precipitate a race by individual fishermen to maximize shares of the total quota, and thus produce shorter and shorter fishing seasons, greater periods of idleness for men and gear, higher freezing, storage, and marketing costs, and unbalanced harvesting of the stocks concerned. If, as in the case of halibut and tuna, real prices have been rising over time, the pressure toward very short seasons and very high costs is exaggerated. The classic case is that of the British Columbia roe herring fishery, which, in a recent year, took its entire quota in the most productive areas in 15 minutes! (This was the time required for each of the hundreds of purse seiners that had gathered at the grounds to make one set.)

If management measures cannot prevent the accumulation of more and more excess capacity in the fishery, it may become difficult or impossible to achieve even limited biological objectives. The margin for error simply becomes too great when the amount of gear in the water is so great that allowable fishing times are measured in hours and days.

Unhappily, one must still comment on the economic absurdity of regulating fisheries subject to overexploitation by restricting the use of the most efficient types of vessel and gear. The impact of such programs on total fishing costs for any given output is obvious. In addition, they tend to drive a wedge between the individual fisherman, who properly resents restrictions on what he knows to be more efficient methods, and the fishery agency which is imposing such restrictions while trying to assist him in other ways. Even more serious is the negative effect of such regulations on the incentive in both government and private industry to undertake research in fishing methods and equipment. It simply makes no sense to waste money on development if success only generates a new set of restrictions on whatever improved techniques or gear result. Yet one finds such restrictions, all clothed in the good name of conservation, in virtually every regulated fishery in the world.

It might be noted, in passing, that restrictions on efficient fishing methods and equipment are frequently the result of pressure on government by one group of fishermen to restrict another rather than conservation measures. Thus, when the State of Alaska restricts salmon purse seiners to 17 meters in length, it is

because such regulation will exclude many of the larger
seiners from the State of Washington from Alaska waters.
Restrictions on the use of purse seines in waters of the
Northeast Atlantic follow the same pattern. The real
reason for prohibiting the use of seiners is usually the
political pressure of those using less efficient gear.

The experience with fisheries under open access or
traditional management in the past can be summarized as
follows:

1. Left to the market alone, any significant commercial fishery will inevitably use too many resources,
frequently in inefficient ways, and may deplete the
resource itself if prices and costs are sufficiently
favorable.

2. Hence, some kind of intervention is essential if
marine fisheries are to return anything approaching the
economic benefit of which they are capable; and in many
cases the very survival of valuable stocks may require
regulation of fishing.

3. This does not mean, however, that regulation is
always the proper answer. The investment required to
develop adequate and scientific understanding of the
species involved is far from trivial; fishery management,
as well as the commercial fishery itself, requires scarce
resources. For many species, therefore, it may be more
sensible to bear the social and economic costs of excessive rates of exploitation than to bear the larger costs
of developing an information system and a management
framework.

4. Management systems based solely on the objective
of protecting fish stocks invariably lead to excessive
costs in the fishery. In the case of very heavily exploited species, it may prove impossible even to achieve
the biological goal if the economic responses of the
regulated fishery are ignored.

5. The problem of open access has international as
well as national dimensions. De facto acceptance worldwide of a 200-mile fishery conservation zone under the
control of the coastal state offers an opportunity to
internalize many of the external costs of an internationally shared fishery, and thus to manage rationally even
if foreign participation is permitted under control of
the coastal state. It must be recognized, however, that
many important marine fish populations are transboundary.
While the number of international participants certainly
is reduced by the extension of coastal state jurisdic-
tion, there remains an urgent need to develop workable
international management systems for stocks that are
accessible to two or more countries.

A BIOECONOMIC APPROACH TO MANAGEMENT

The consensus among virtually all resource economists who have looked into the problems of fishery
management is that regulation of the traditional type,
while frequently successful in preserving threatened
resources and therefore preserving future options, has
done little to improve economic benefits and promote
growth of a viable commercial fishing industry. Most of
us, then, are looking for techniques which do as well or
better at protecting fishery stocks, but which work
through rather than against the market mechanism. Ideally, of course, we would like to find an avenue through
which the system of private property rights and competitive markets which has served us well in so many other
areas could be made applicable to the fisheries. Unfortunately, the obstacles to such a simple (or simplistic)
approach are formidable. But it does seem possible to
improve the regulatory process greatly by providing the
individual fisherman with incentives to behave in a
fashion which seems rational to him and which simultaneously achieves most of the objectives outlined above for
an adequately protected and reasonably efficient fishery.
Three techniques are available to achieve these objectives: the use of taxes or fees to make explicit to
the individual fisherman the external costs that he im-
poses on other fishermen by thinning of stocks or by
crowding on favored fishing grounds; controlling the number of fishing vessels or fishermen (or both) under a
limited licensing scheme; or limiting the total catch by
quota and further subdividing this into individual quotas
assigned to individual fishermen and tradeable on the
market.
In a world of completely static conditions, with all
yields known perfectly in advance, with the capacity to
forecast prices at all periods of time, and with no
changes in the biological system that determines the
availability of desired species, any one of these three
techniques could produce an economically optimal fishery.
(For a formal exposition, see Clark, 1977, 1980.) Unfortunately, we have now determined that none of these conditions can hold in the real world. Accordingly, the
suitability of these techniques (or of more than one in
parallel) must be judged on other bases. Are they technically feasible? Do they provide adequate flexibility
to insure productivity of the stocks in the event of
radical, unforeseen changes in the populations exploited?
Can they be enforced at reasonable cost and with a minimum of irritation to the fishing industry? Do they
induce fishermen to use efficient gear in efficient numbers in their own self-interest? Do they provide the
incentive for continued research and development which

will further improve the economic contribution of the
industry?

Taxes or Fees

The use of taxes (or fees or royalties) to control
the level of fishing effort is designed to equalize private and social costs. Under free access each fisherman
inflicts "external costs" on others since his operations
reduce the availability of fish and raise the costs of
other fishermen; but such costs do not show up in his
accounting. The various types of externalities associated with open access fishing--reduction of stocks,
crowding, and incompatible types of gear--can all be cor-
rected, in theory, by imposing taxes that reflect the
full social cost of the operation rather than the direct
costs of fishing as seen by the operator himself. The
fishery could then be left to the market, without direct
intervention by government. The combination of factor
costs and taxes would induce each fisherman to adopt the
best combination of vessel, equipment, and labor.

Unfortunately, the theoretical neatness of this
solution is hopelessly out of line with the realities of
practical fishing operations. It rests on the assumption
that fisheries operate in a completely static world in
which outputs, costs, prices, and fishermen's behavior
are either constant or can be forecast accurately over
the planning horizon of the fishing enterprise. Nothing
could be farther from the truth, of course. All commercial fisheries are subject to tremendously wide variations in yield-effort relations and therefore in both
short-term and long-term costs. For most fisheries the
"right" level of catch must vary from year to year, sometimes over wide ranges. Very few governments will allow
an administrative agency the authority to vary taxes over
an equally wide range. And even if they did, it is far
from certain that taxes could be adjusted in a manner
that would produce the desired level of fishing effort as
rapidly as biological circumstances dictate.

The weakness of the tax approach is particularly
acute in the case of a fishery that has already become
heavily over-capitalized. To reduce the amount of fishing capacity to a level consistent with resource capabilities and efficient use of all vessels and gear would
require a tax sufficient to reduce vessel earnings below
variable or out-of-pocket costs. The cut would have to
be even deeper than in most industries, since the payments to labor are normally paid on a share basis in a
fishing enterprise. This means that the impact of a tax
on earnings of the vessel owner would be reduced by
shifting a portion of it to the labor force. To achieve
any real reduction in excess capacity would require a tax
heavy enough to put every fisherman in a loss position.

The job of standing before a group of fishermen and ex-
plaining how such a program will solve their problems is
not attractive!

This does not mean that taxes cannot and should not
be used to shape incentive in ways that supplement other
programs to reduce or prevent over-investment in fisheries. In particular, a tax on landings, representing a
proxy for a tax on fishing effort, could be used effectively to cover the cost of research and management programs, and to capture some of the benefits to those
programs for the general public. It could also contribute usefully both to better allocation of resources by
nudging fishermen in the proper direction with respect to
vessels and gear employed and total effort. But taxes
simply cannot be used as a short-run adjustment mechanism
whenever fluctuations in natural abundance dictate a
change in allowable catch. These must be handled by
other fast-response measures that can be used to close
down or curtail fishing whenever unexpected developments
pose serious resource problems.

Controlling Inputs: Limited Entry Programs

A more realistic approach to more efficient management, now coming into fairly common usage, is to control
inputs to the fishery by limiting the number of fishing
units. This could be done by controlled licensing either
of fishermen or fishing vessels, but in practice it has
proved more effective to license vessels--the primary
unit of the fishing enterprise. For any desired level of
catch, it appears relatively simple to determine the number of optimal vessels of proper size and properly
equipped, required to take that catch during an average
year.

In practice, limited entry programs are much more
complicated in operation. Normally the pressure to adopt
such a program rarely comes before the industry is already heavily over-capitalized, and discussion of the
intention to establish a limited entry program always
leads to a rush of new entrants to establish position in
the industry before the number of licenses is frozen.
Thus, there is invariably a great deal of excess capacity
to deal with from the outset.

This can be minimized in several ways. One is to
establish criteria for eligibility for the limited
licenses that exclude many of the inactive units and late
entrants. For example, the cutoff date for active vessels to establish eligibility could be set back far
enough to eliminate many of the last minute entrants, and
minimum landing requirements could serve to weed out inactive licensees. The importance of cutting back excess
capacity as far as possible at the outset of the program
cannot be overemphasized. Unless this is done, every

licensed unit, no matter how small its contribution to
the fishery, has the potential to become an active, well-
equipped, modern fishing unit. Thus, even if the number
of licensees is held constant, the actual fishing power
of the fleet could continue to increase substantially as
less productive vessels are up-graded.

A second and tougher approach to the problem of cutting back the number of licensed units in a limited entry
program would be to auction the initial number of licenses desired. While this might present obvious political difficulties, particularly if the number of unsuccessful bidders will be large, it does follow the old
political adage: If one must eat a bad meal, it is best
not to do it one bite at a time.

In a more serious vein, the idea of auctioning to
deal with the initial distribution of rights has much to
recommend it. In the first place, it has a selective
tendency toward efficiency. The highest bids are likely
to come from the most skilled and best equipped fishermen. Second, it by-passes the difficult distributional
problem of bestowing upon people who happen to be in the
right place at the right time valuable property rights in
a publicly owned resource. Finally, it gives fishery management more latitude in the use of other regulatory
techniques if the threat of excess capacity in the fishery is minimized at the outset. Opposition to this
"brute force" approach to reduction of excess capacity
could be reduced by compensating unsuccessful bidders who
had a record of active participation in the fishery from
the proceeds of the auction. (They would still be able
to participate in the fishery, of course, by buying a
license from a successful bidder.)

Once established in the possession of fishermen,
limited licenses become a fairly conventional type of
property, the value of which would depend on the extent
to which the number of fishing vessels in the operation
had been reduced, and the resulting increase in expected
future incomes of the remaining license holders. Although some programs of license limitation have specified
that the licenses be nontransferable, presumably to prevent speculative gains to the initial holders, there are
persuasive arguments for making them freely transferable.
The most significant advantage would be the flexibility
that would be achieved in permitting exit from or entry
to the industry and the freedom of individual license
holders to dispose of their right as they see fit (i.e.,
by sale, lease, bequest to children, etc.). The prices
of the licenses would provide a highly useful barometer
of the economic health of the fishery. And, perhaps most
important, since the going price of a license would
represent the opportunity cost of the right to go fishing, there would be continuing pressure for the licenses
to go to the most efficient operators.

It is difficult to conceive of any government-administered program that could handle the allocation of fishing rights as efficiently as an organized market in licenses. Experience in Australia, Canada, and the United States confirms the expectation that an active market for fishing licenses will develop quickly, and that attempts to restrict transferability of licenses are usually ineffective, since there are innumerable ways of getting around such limitations.

If it seems too difficult, for political or social reasons, to reduce the number of active licenses at the beginning of a limited entry program, the full economic benefits of license limitation can be realized only by some type of "buy-back program," under which government purchases and retires licenses (and perhaps vessels as well). Theoretically, there is no reason why a buy-back program could not be made self-financing, with taxes on the remaining licensees (who gain from each reduction in active vessels) providing the funds for repurchase of licenses.

Experience in other countries reveals some difficulties with this approach, however. Unless reduction in the number of licenses is accompanied by increasing taxes on those remaining, the capitalized value of the remaining licenses will increase, and prices asked for them will quickly exhaust the resources of the buy-back program. But unless it was announced at the beginning of the program that progressive tax increases would be levied, the holders of licenses are likely to argue vigorously (with some justification) that they have been expropriated in part. Their investments in licenses and vessels, undertaken in good faith, could be expected to yield only a competitive rate of return. If a tax is now levied on license holders to finance a buy-back program, existing license holders will find their property rights sharply reduced in value and current earnings will fall below the rate of return anticipated when the license was purchased. It is not surprising, then, that buy-back programs in countries that have attempted to reduce excessive fishing capacity in this fashion have come to an abrupt halt before they had achieved any significant results.

In short, buy-back programs can be used to reduce the number of licenses to any desired level in a limited entry program, but it is nearly impossible to do so without specifying in advance the level of taxation on remaining licensees that will be required to service the program. It is unlikely, and, in general principle, undesirable, that a buy-back program be financed out of general tax revenues. It would therefore be most desirable to reduce unnecessary capacity as much as possible at the outset of a limited entry program, either by auctioning licenses initially or by establishing restrictive criteria on eligibility. It must also be specified in advance that the holders of valuable rights to use the public domain will be expected to pay for that privilege.

It goes without saying that if a buy-back program is utilized to reduce the number of licenses and vessels participating in the fishery, the redundant capacity must not be permitted to enter other fisheries that require management.

Another major problem with limited entry programs is the difficulty in preventing increases in fishing power and/or increases in unnecessary capital investment on individual fishing vessels. In theory, with an active market for licenses, one would expect the average vessel to earn an average competitive rate of return, with the capitalized value of the license representing the cost that must be incurred in order to enjoy a portion of the economic rent that the fishery can generate. If all fishermen could foresee all consequences of their actions, it would also follow that each would adopt the most efficient factor combination possible--that is, the best size, equipment, and seasonal and area deployment of the vessel.

Unfortunately, the apparent self-interest of the individual fisherman is likely to lead him in other directions--to the considerable detriment of the efficiency of the fleet as a whole. In the simplest case, this simply means upgrading less productive licensed units. To the extent that the upgrading brings the vessel and gear closer to optimal configuration in terms of today's technology, the efficiency of the individual unit might well improve, but the total level of effort would again be excessive. This could be controlled only by undertaking further reduction in the number of licenses.

More serious is the perceived opportunity of an individual fisherman to expand his share of the catch by increasing the fishing power of his vessel in a variety of ways (e.g., increased engine capacity, more electronic equipment to permit fishing in rougher weather, increased number of crewmen in order to handle gear faster). As long as the value of the expected increment to catch exceeded the additional private cost of the added equipment, the individual fisherman would regard himself as better off even though the resulting combination of inputs produced higher average costs of production.

But this process would obviously be self-defeating for the fleet as a whole. Everyone will obviously play the same game--indeed, each fisherman may be forced to do so in order to "protect" his share of the catch. The end result is again excessive fishing power, higher costs of operation for each individual vessel, and a reduction in aggregate fleet efficiency. In effect, if the only unit controlled is the vessel itself, a variation of "new entry" becomes possible in the form of added inputs used with the vessel. Even if this could be controlled (for example, by limiting not only the number of vessels but the length, horsepower, tonnage or other dimensions of the individual vessel) there is almost certain to be some margin within which the self-defeating process described above would take place. (See Pearse and Wilen, 1979.)

How important this effect may be is an empirical matter. In some fisheries, the technological nature of the harvesting operation may dictate a fixed combination of inputs, and any attempt to alter this would result in very rapid increases in costs. In other cases, the encouragement of wasteful capital inputs to try to "catch yours before the hoarders do" could assume really serious proportions. Any thorough effort to control the process would run the risk of freezing the fishery to a given technology, which would certainly tend to discourage technical development and innovation.

An appraisal of the effectiveness of limited entry programs around the world reveals wide variations. In the prawn fishery of South Australia, the number of fishing vessels was limited by law even before the fishery had begun to develop. As a result, even though the ingenuity of Australian fishermen produced some astonishing increases in the catching power of the licensed vessels, the limited numbers of licensees were able to harvest all allowable prawn at remarkably low costs. The few licenses that had been transferred under that program indicated that very substantial economic rents were being earned.

By contrast, a limited entry program introduced after widespread development of the northern prawn fisheries of Australia had to contend with more than 800 existing vessels, whose aggregate catch was only about 3 or 4 times that of the 50 South Australian prawn fishermen.

In the salmon fisheries of British Columbia, it has been pointed out that much of the otherwise substantial economic gain from reducing the number of vessels from approximately 7,500 to 5,000 through a license control and buy-back program has been dissipated by excessive investment in new hulls, high-speed propulsion units, elaborate electronic gear, etc. Strangely, this process has not taken place to any noticeable degree in either Alaska or the State of Washington, both of which have had limited entry programs in salmon fishing for a number of years.

A bit of caution must be noted in interpreting the data on "excessive" investment in the individual vessel under limited entry programs. For example, analysis of the British Columbia data indicated that a major part of the "wasteful" investment was in electronic equipment which is standard aboard fishing vessels of many

developed countries, and which reflects a justifiable
concern by the fisherman with his own safety at sea.
Similarly, many fishermen live aboard their vessels (or
at least spend a great deal of time aboard them), and
some of the additional expenditures reflect the desire
for a more comfortable life aboard--something that would
not have been possible until the limited entry program
improved incomes to the point where the fisherman had
access to the capital market through normal channels. If
this "capital stuffing" tendency does become serious, the
most obvious remedy would be a tax on landings which
would sharply reduce the perceived advantage of trying to
expand one's share of a given catch.

Finally, it should be reiterated that a limited
entry program can, even under ideal circumstances, only
provide the correct number of vessels for an average
situation. It is not a flexible weapon for dealing with
short-run fluctuations in abundance and availability of
fish, and would have to be supplemented by direct controls over fishing to meet emergencies.

With that kind of support, a limited entry program,
coupled with a stable or gradually increasing landings
tax, could do much to move any marine fishery in the
direction of more rational exploitation, though it would
still fall short of ideal performance in economic terms.
It does, of course, enjoy the great advantage of being a
relatively simple and straightforward technique which
could be instituted with a minimum of disturbance to the
industry.

Controlling Output: Individual Fish Quotas

Another alternative would be to attack the open access problem by controlling the individual fishermen's
outputs rather than inputs. This would involve the creation of a specified number of individual rights to a
given quantity of fish (individual fish quotas), tied to
an overall quota, rather than a property right to go
fishing, with the quantity unspecified. In practice,
of course, it would probably be necessary to define the
individual fish quota in terms of a percentage of the
overall quota rather than an absolute number, since total
catch quotas for most fisheries would be changed from
season to season.

Although the attractiveness of the proposal may stem
from the fact that it has never been tried in practice
and therefore is free of the "bugs" already known to
plague limited entry and tax programs, it does have some
intriguing advantages. Not the least of these is the
certainty of its control over each season's catch. Once
the overall quota is determined, the sum of the individual fish quotas is also determined, and the possibility
of wide variations from expected catches can be

minimized. It achieves that tight control without invit-
ing behavior that results in seriously inefficient operation under a single overall quota.

The most important advantage of this approach is the
freedom it allows the fisherman to make his own choice of
vessel, gear, area, and time of fishing. There is no
reason why more than minimal government interference
would be required if the overall quota is properly chosen
and if the individual quotas are tightly enforced. Since
each operator would have a firm entitlement to a given
amount of fish each year, depending on the number of quotas he had been issued initially or had acquired, the
decision to pursue a single fishery or equip his vessel
for multi-fishery operation could be left to the individual's own choice. Unlike other management systems, control over individual fishing quotas would encourage the
development of better gear and techniques, since they
would add to the individual fisherman's earnings without
increasing pressure on the resource.

Initial allocation of individual quotas would present no more difficulty than initial allocation of fishing licenses, and--like licenses--the quotas, once
issued, could become permanent, freely transferable
rights. Since the inherent flexibility of the system
could be realized only if fairly easy and costless transfers of quotas could be achieved both within seasons and
between seasons, development of mechanisms for orderly
transfer of quotas would be a first priority in initi-
ating the program. There seems little doubt that an
active market for these rights would arise quickly, although some government assistance in "making the market"
might be required initially. If quotas are freely trans-
ferrable the program would avoid the serious drawbacks to
fixed catch limits for each vessel: the inherent penalty
to more energetic and skilled fishermen, and the restriction on incentives for innovation.

Indeed, it is difficult to find serious disadvantages with the proposal, at least on the theoretical
level. In practice, of course, there are bound to be
some difficulties. Perhaps the most important relates to
enforcement. Experience everywhere with landings taxes
demonstrates the ease with which under-reporting can
develop. Since both buyer and seller may also have incentives for under-reporting under a fish quota system,
the problem of maintaining control over quota catches and
the integrity of the basic data system on which fishery
management rests might be compromised.

No less important, in many respects, is the attitude
of fishermen themselves. Fishermen are among the most
conservative groups in the world, and it is unlikely that
they would look on an entirely different system of fishery management with any great enthusiasm. A system of
individual fish quotas, which would involve a complete

change in the way fishermen plan their initial investments and their year-to-year changes in vessels, gear,
and fishing strategies is likely to be viewed with more
than usual suspicion. Obviously, these difficulties are
not insuperable; they simply suggest that a major effort
would have to be made to meet with fishermen throughout
the areas affected and explain, carefully and in as much
detail as possible, the meaning of the new program and
its effect on individual operators. Common sense would
also suggest that the initial fishery picked to test the
program should be relatively simple in structure, carried
on by well-organized, businesslike operators, and not
subject to excessive economic or biological stress. It
would be far easier to extend the scheme to more difficult fisheries with a success story in hand.

SOME PROBLEMS AND NONPROBLEMS WITH RATIONALIZATION
PROGRAMS

Distribution Effects

We now turn to a number of problems (and nonproblems) that would arise under any management scheme aimed
at economic rationalization of heavily exploited fisheries. The first concerns distribution effects. I find
it difficult to generate much concern about adverse distribution effects of a properly designed limited entry
or individual fish quota program. The changes induced
in regional income distribution by limited changes in a
small part of the total labor force are not likely to
bulk large as public issues. Indeed, the most serious
distribution conflicts are likely to come from disagree-
ments over shares of the catch by groups of fishermen
from different areas or using different types of gear.
If a restricted entry or individual quota system
were accompanied by appropriate tax measures, it seems
most unlikely that unacceptable differentials in income
between those remaining in the fishery and other sectors
of the fishing industry would arise. It is even less
likely that economically rational fishery management
would create unacceptably large windfalls to fishermen
vis-a-vis other workers in the economy. Indeed, one of
the objectives of a fishery management program that produces improved economic performance should be to bring
fishermen's incomes back to a parity with those of other
groups. As indicated earlier, one of the sad commen-
taries on the existing state of fishery management is the
general tendency for fishermen's incomes to lag behind
the rest of the economy, even when biologically effective
controls have been instituted.

Creation of Monopoly Power

Various methods of restricting inputs by creating
property rights in fisheries have often been criticized
as monopolistic in effect. Usually this reflects simple
ignorance of the mechanics of such programs. To the extent that licenses or fish quotas are freely transfer-
rable and available to anyone, fisheries are no more
closed to new entry than agriculture, forestry, or any
other industry in which one must acquire a right to use a
natural resource before he can participate.

It is possible that limiting entry to a fishery, by
whatever means, might enable fishermen to offer counter-
vailing power to the persistent tendency toward monopsony
or oligopsony in waterfront markets for fish. But surely
this would be an advantage rather than a disadvantage,
since the possibility of bilateral action by fishermen
and buyers to exploit the general public would be remote
indeed. Anyone who has worked closely with fishermen
would agree that they are probably the most unlikely
group of monopolistic conspirators that one could find.

Effects on Small-Scale and Part-Time Fishermen

A more serious set of problems arises from the
social impact of limited entry programs on small, part-
time fishermen, particularly those living in isolated
areas where alternative employment opportunities are
severely limited. It is certainly possible that either
limited licenses or limited numbers of fish quotas would
be bid up to levels that would exclude many of these
fishermen--not necessarily on the basis of economic efficiency, but rather on the basis of better access to capital, better business organization, and the ability to
operate in more than one fishery. To the extent that the
problem is simply one of providing better financial services, it could be dealt with in conventional fashion--
through government loan assistance or the formation of
vigorous cooperative organizations. But where efficiency
in the fishery calls for a significant reduction in the
number of fishermen and there are, literally, no alternative types of employment to which they can turn, social
considerations may dictate modification of economic objectives. It may be possible to achieve social goals for
coastal communities more efficiently by utilizing more
people in the fishery than are required than through any
other type of program. But it must be stressed that this
argument has often been misused to dodge the difficult
problems of regional development. It is easier to hide
unemployment in isolated fishing communities by sloppy
administration of fishery programs than to undertake more
difficult regional economic programs to increase mobility
and employment opportunities.

A related but separable problem concerns part-time fishermen. There are many parts of the world in which part-time fishing is undertaken as a logical complementary activity to seasonal farming, logging, or other occupations. It is quite possible that a limited license program, for example, might impose an insuperable barrier to continuance of this type of operation. The part-time operator could not afford to bid as high as an operator engaged full-time or nearly full-time in a single fishery. A program of individual fish quotas would be much more flexible in this respect.

Effects on Secondary Activities

There may be a hue and cry about reducing employment in boat-building and other service industries related to the fishery if the amount of excess gear in the water is reduced. But surely secondary as well as primary activities associated with excessively large capital investment in the fishery are equally wasteful. To the extent that service activities simply support idle capacity, reducing them is clearly in the national interest. No one in his right mind would argue that these adjustments can be achieved overnight, in the service sector any more than in the fishery itself; but neither can it be argued that the nation benefits by perpetuating unnecessary capacity indefinitely.

Effects on Fishermen's Way of Life

Even less convincing is the argument that insistence on economic efficiency as an objective of fishery management is invalid because it does not take into consideration the nonmonetary satisfactions derived from the lifestyle associated with commercial fishing. It is true that fishing tends to attract highly individualistic people who derive a great deal of satisfaction from association with the sea, but precisely the same argument could be made with respect to a host of other occupations. Teaching, farming, professional, and managerial work, and the entertainment world come to mind as examples. Indeed, one of the most undesirable aspects of an open access fishery is that casual participants make it difficult or impossible for a dedicated and truly professional fisherman to make a decent living. There is no particular reason why those to whom fishing is a particularly appealing way of life should not also eat regularly and live in some comfort.

GENERAL COMMENTS ON FISHERY DEVELOPMENT

   The preceding discussion was general in nature,
though the basic conclusions are applicable in most countries with marine fisheries. In the sections that follow
we discuss some problems of application that may have
particular relevance to American coastal states.

Interaction of Industrial and Artisanal Fisheries

   Almost every country in the world, developing or
developed, faces potential conflicts in policy in dealing
with industrial and artisanal fisheries. Industrial
fisheries, as the name implies, are expected to utilize
state-of-the-art technology to provide a large and continuing flow of raw materials to meet domestic protein
food demands and/or to earn foreign exchange through export of semi-processed or processed fish products. While
development of the artisanal fisheries is also expected
to benefit protein food supplies to some extent, the
major thrust of government policy is usually toward upgrading of living standards, improved access to education
and other social services, and increased mobility of the
population to relieve chronic under-employment. The
problems of the artisanal fisheries are commonly part of
a much wider challenge of regional economic stagnation,
limited employment opportunities, and cultural and geographic isolation that produces strong resistance to
economic or social change.
   There is no reason why different policies cannot be
developed for these rather different kinds of fishing
industries, and experience in many parts of the world
demonstrates that it is possible to do so without conflict or inconsistency. But the traps are numerous.
Perhaps the most serious is the possibility that industrial fishing operations will impinge on stocks that are
directly or indirectly basic to the artisanal fisheries.
It is also possible that rapid development of industrial
operations for fresh and frozen fish may preempt local
and regional markets previously served by artisanal
fisheries. The small boat operator is simply forced out
of these markets or faced with significantly lower
prices.
   It might also be noted that upgrading artisanal
fisheries normally means the introduction of more capital
intensive techniques, and it is possible that the demand
for labor will actually decline. Unless such development
programs are undertaken in the context of a sensible and
productive regional economic development program, with
emphasis on labor mobility, fishery development can
create as many social problems as it solves in coastal
communities.

Management and Marketing

Although the general discussion above centered on the economic aspects of the harvesting activity and its management, these can never be divorced from processing and marketing considerations. In particular, a major marine fishery whose products are sold in international trade faces special requirements that impinge on the managing agency. It is axiomatic that a fishery competing in international markets must be managed in a way which emphasizes economic efficiency. These markets are now so well-organized and competitive that sloppy operations are simply not viable. The international market also places stringent demands on the industry, at every stage from harvesting through physical distribution, with respect to the quality and uniformity of its products. The effect of regulations geared solely to the protection of fish stocks can lead a perfectly rational fishing enterprise to operate in ways that seriously compromise the quality of fish delivered to the dock--and, inevitably, the quality of the final products. Thus, a simple overall quota system provides a strong incentive for the individual fisherman to make only full trips back from the fishing grounds; an early return to port with a partial load (to protect quality) will rarely permit another complete trip to the grounds before the quota is filled. The result: wide variations in the quality of fish delivered to the processor, and adverse market reaction. The Pacific halibut, Pacific salmon, and even the tuna fishery have had problems of this sort.

Marketing also becomes a part of the overall fishery management problem if monopsony or oligopsony in waterfront markets results in noncompetitive prices to fishermen. The situation is common throughout world fisheries. Small fishing boats are notoriously uneconomic carriers over any distance, thus limiting the size of primary market areas. Since the optimal scale of waterfront receiving/processing facilities, though small, is large enough relative to these local markets to rule out the existence of a large number of buyers, noncompetitive behavior is likely.

To identify the problem is one thing; to do something about it is quite another. Although artisanal fishermen complain constantly about exploitive behavior by middlemen, usually with some justification, there are other important elements to be considered; there is, afterall, a difference between "expensive" and "excessive." Fishermen, the general public, and governments are likely to conclude, uncritically, that a wide gap between prices paid to fishermen and prices in retail markets must mean excessive margins for middlemen. But fish are expensive products to handle in commerce, particularly where landings are scattered along a coast

characterized by difficult transportation and communication. At best, marketing of fish is a nerve-wracking
management problem, demanding constant attention to product quality, continuity of supply, and full utilization
of specialized transport, storage, and freezing facilities.

In addition, waterfront marketers frequently undertake the function of financing fishermen on a broader
basis than the usual banker/business relationship. Middlemen may not only provide funds for equipping and
operating fishing vessels, but also for "income maintenance" during off seasons; to meet the cost of lost vessels and gear; or to deal with matters related to the
fisherman's personal life. Whatever the motives of the
marketer may be, the functions performed are vitally important in artisanal fisheries, particularly in isolated
locations. Any policy designed to introduce new channels
of distribution to reduce monopsonistic influences must
be carefully tailored to provide for real needs now met,
however imperfectly, by middlemen.

Cooperatives have been employed successfully as a
means of mitigating the effects of buyer control over
fishermen. The record, however, is mixed. It has been
particularly spotty where the formation of cooperatives
has become an active government policy, carried on by an
agency whose success is judged largely by the number of
cooperatives formed.

The cooperative is one of the most difficult and
complex of all types of business organization, particularly when it must deal with highly perishable products
such as fish. Successful operations have been characterized, almost without exception, by three things: superi-
or management; the ability to integrate marketing of fish
and the cooperative provision of inputs required by fishermen; and the ability to finance these activities
through links to broader regional and national cooperative movements. Successful cooperatives also require a
kind of mental attitude in the community affected that
accepts the principles of cooperation and the discipline
that must go with it. Where the formation of cooperatives has become an end in itself, the temptation to impose high-cost cooperatives on fishermen by requiring
that all fish be marketed through the coop or similar
constraints has been all too common.

What To Do With 200 Miles of Water

A rather different kind of national fishery management policy concerns the disposition to be made of the
new coastal state authority over living resources within
200 miles. Most nations seem to take it for granted that
it is economically advantageous to develop a domestic
flag fishery as rapidly as possible, and to displace all

foreign fishing within the coastal zone. The fact that policies designed to accelerate the pace of that displacement frequently run counter to the nation's own broader international trade policy (and its own well-being) seems to receive surprisingly little attention.

The greatest increase in national well-being for a coastal state may come from development of domestic fishing capacity up to the limits of resource capabilities with the control zone, but that is certainly not an automatic finding. Expansion of a domestic fleet involves additional inputs, much of it in the form of demands on an already scarce supply of capital. While it may utilize otherwise unemployed people, experience suggests the opposite--many of those who will build and operate the new fleets will be skilled or semi-skilled people already productively employed. Clearly, the advantages to any nation of expanding its own share of the fishery resources within its 200-mile limit must be based on a careful calculation of net economic benefit, appropriately discounted to present values, and modified as necessary to account for the impact of such a program on pockets of unemployment and other social aspects of the fishing community.

From this point of view, there are a number of other alternatives that deserve serious consideration. For example, many of the less developed nations can obtain much larger economic benefits, including foreign exchange earnings, by straight rental arrangements with foreign operators of high seas fishing vessels (accompanied, in some cases, by a scheduled phase-out of foreign operations in the future). This is particularly likely to be advantageous for countries with very limited port facilities or where otherwise good fishing ports are badly lacking in essential infrastructure. A variation of this policy might link access to the coastal state's fisheries to nonfishery investments in the coastal state, access to the distant water operator's home markets, training of domestic workers in a variety of skills (fishing and non-fishing); and combinations of these economically valuable services.

In many cases the joint venture, a form of business organization which had acquired a distinctly dubious reputation after World War II, may offer profitable opportunities for both parties in the new setting in which the coastal state holds the trump card--access to the resources. Apart from its obvious advantage of providing capital and expertise that may be lacking in the coastal state, it can also open much wider markets and can shorten significantly the learning period required for coastal state fishermen and processors to become competent in the operation. The joint venture is particularly attractive in the present economic setting. Distant water operators such as Japan, Korea, and the USSR, forced out of many of their traditional fishing areas, have substantial excess capacity in modern factory ships and processing vessels that may be obtained, via the joint venture, at far lower cost than if the coastal state had to produce, or purchase, and staff the vessels.

Finally, coastal states might well consider the possibility of competitive bidding for all or a portion of the sustainable yield over and above the capacity of its domestic industry to utilize. The international market for fish is sufficiently strong and diverse to provide reasonable assurance that bidding would be competitive. The resulting prices for fish quotas would provide a more accurate measure than now exists of the net economic value of access to controlled resources, and a valuable benchmark against which to evaluate other development alternatives for the coastal state.

A FINAL PLEA FOR APPLIED SCIENCE AND DATA SYSTEMS

In closing, I would emphasize again, as strongly as possible, the over-riding importance of information systems and assessment capability if programs of fishery development and regulation are to succeed.

There are two reasons for emphasizing stock assessment and monitoring so strongly. First, there is an inherent tendency for an expanding fishing industry, utilizing a previously untouched or lightly fished stock, to over-estimate long-term yield capabilities. In the early flush years of any new fishery the boats will be harvesting an accumulated stock of larger individuals; but this must inevitably be followed by a decline in catch per unit effort as the fishery settles down to sustainable catch levels. Second, while very few marine fish populations can actually be fished to extinction, many can be reduced by commercial fishing to levels at which species substitution occurs. Reversion to the initial stock situation may not occur even though fishing effort on the valuable target species is curtailed. Finally, the economic cost of rebuilding a depleted stock is a serious matter. Even very rapidly growing species such as tuna may take two or three years of severely curtailed fishing to reach the initial level from which recovery starts. For long-lived, slow-growing species, the recovery period may extend as long as fifteen or twenty years, even with sharp reductions in fishing effort and catch. In short, the risks in plunging ahead with fishery development programs without adequate knowledge of the dynamics of the population under exploitation are so great as to suggest a very conservative policy with respect to the pace of development and a firm policy of building the scientific capacity to assess and monitor those stocks.

32

SELECTED READINGS

Anderson, L. G. (ed.). Economic Impacts of Extended
    Fisheries Jurisdiction. Ann Arbor: Ann Arbor Science,
    1977.
_____. The Economics of Fisheries Management.
    Baltimore: The Johns Hopkins University Press, 1977.
_____. "A Comparison of Limited Entry Fisheries
    Management Schemes." Report of the ACMRR Working
    Party on the Scientific Basis of Determining Manage-
    ment Measures, FAO Fisheries Report No. 236, 1979.
Bell, F. W. "Technological Externalities and Common
    Property Resources: An Empirical Study of the U.S.
    Northern Lobster Fishery." Journal of Political
    Economy 80, 1972.
Brown, G. L., Jr. "An Optimal Program of Managing Common
    Property Resources with Congention Externalities."
    Journal of Political Economy 82, 1974.
Christy, F. T. "Fisherman Catch Quotas." Ocean Division,
    International Law Journal 1, 1973.
Clark, C. W. Mathematical Bioeconomics: The Optimal Con-
    trol of Renewable Resources. New York: John Wiley,
    Interscience.
_____. "Towards a Predictive Model for the Economic
    Regulation of Commercial Fisheries." Canadian Journal
    of Fisheries and Aquatic Sciences 37, No. 7, 1980.
Crutchfield, J. A. "An Economic Evaluation of Alternative
    Methods of Fishery Regulation." Journal of Law and
    Economics 4, 1961.
_____. "Economic and Political Objectives in
    Fishery Management." Transactions of the American
    Fisheries Society 102, 1973.
Pearse, P. H. and J. E. Wilen. "Impact of Canada's
    Pacific Salmon Fleet Control Program." Journal of the
    Fisheries Research Board of Canada 36, 1979.
Stokes, R. L. "Limitation of Fishing Effort: An Economic
    Analysis of Options." Marine Policy 3, No. 3, 1979.

3
Forest Policy

Marion Clawson and Roger A. Sedjo

INTRODUCTION
    The economic and social importance of forests in the
lives of people in any region or nation is coming increasingly to be recognized in many countries of the world.
The availability of forests, long taken for granted in
many parts of the world, is dependent on public and private actions now and in the future. The role of forests
in any country depends upon its natural endowments for
forests, the state of its economic development, and upon
national aspirations and goals for the life of the people.
    There exists today in the world a large number of
different forest situations. Without attempting a complete cataloguing of those numerous situations, the following type situations may be identified as relevant to
the discussion here. Each of these calls for a different
kind of public policy and for different private actions,
if the full economic and social values of the forests are
to be realized.
    First of all, there are countries or large regions
of countries with relatively poor or limited forests
where wood for fuel is basic and scarce. Some such countries are arid, and never had generous forests; others
have exploited their forests in the past, and today have
only very limited supplies of wood. In some countries,
the problem is at least partly a matter of transportation,
since there are reasonably good forests in some regions
but a severe shortage of fuel in other regions. Many
countries with such limited forest resources are poor and
the people are highly dependent on wood for fuel to cook
food and to heat homes. It may safely be asserted that a
very large part of the world does indeed have this situation and this problem. Forestry is highly important under these conditions, but it is not the kind of forestry
which is glamorous or attractive to professionally trained foresters.
    Secondly, there are the temperate zone countries, in
both northern and southern hemispheres, which have or

33

can readily establish softwood forests of native or exotic species, and which have high commercial potential for forestry. The United States and Canada in the Northern Hemisphere fall in this category, as do the Scandanavian and western European countries--even Russia, although much of the latter's forests are so remote and have such low biological productive potential that their commercial potential is limited. In the Southern Hemisphere, New Zealand, Australia, Chile, and perhaps other countries should be included in this group. These countries are also large consumers of forest products. Some of them buy wood products from other countries, some of them sell to other countries.

It is in these temperate regions that most present professional forest knowledge and expertise developed. In general, these are countries with high incomes per capita, where wood is used for many purposes but not primarily for fuel.

Finally, there are tropical and semi-tropical zone countries which had extensive natural forests some years ago, some of which have been cleared for farming or other uses, some of which are still standing but likely to be cleared in the next few decades. These forests have their own particular characteristics, both as standing forests and as objects of commercial exploitation. The clearing of such forests has aroused much concern among ecologists and others. Clearing sets in motion a train of ecological events which is often severely damaging to the area; natural forest reproduction is often slow or nonexistent and planting is often difficult, expensive, and unsuccessful. Even if one decries the clearing of such forests, one must recognize that such clearing has already taken place and that much more is highly probable. For many such areas, the forest policy choice does not lie between preservation and clearing, but upon what to do with areas previously cleared. For these, tree planting, perhaps with exotics, often is the most practical program from both a commercial and an ecological viewpoint.

In some tropic zone countries around the world there are areas where exotic tree species have been or might be introduced for commercial forestry, on lands which are not now and perhaps never were in forests. For such areas, the introduction of exotic tree species from other regions has many similarities to the introduction of exotic farm food and fiber crops. Almost all of the world's food and fiber today comes from crops not native to the regions where they are now grown. Wheat, maize, oats, barley, rice, yams, most of the tree fruits and vegetables, cotton, flax, and other fibers are all "exotics" or imports into most of the regions where they are now grown. The ubiquity of exotics in food and fiber production is not, of course, proof that exotics can be equally successful in forestry, but such experience is suggestive--to economists if not to ecologists.

On a worldwide long historical basis, forestry in the world today is in transition, comparable in general terms to the transition agriculture has gone through over the millenia since it began. At first, man was a hunter-gatherer, finding and utilizing the materials which grew naturally. Much forestry is still in this stage. The next stage was the beginning of cultivation-- the planting of seeds or of plants, at least some minimum care and protection of the growing plants from their enemies and from various risks, a planned harvest with planned utilization of the outputs, and some concern for the next generation of plants. Forestry in some countries has long been like this, and it is becoming more so in some other countries. A third general stage is the application of science or organized knowledge to the selection or breeding of crops and livestock, the establishment of plantations by seeding or by transplanting seedlings, the care and thinning of the plants to take full advantage of the productivity of the site, still more careful harvesting and protection of the harvested material, and still more concern for the next generation of crops by seed selection and preservation. Agriculture around the world is rapidly entering this stage; forestry in many areas is also entering the similar stage. One should not, of course, push this analogy too far, but it is, we think, highly suggestive for forestry.

One aspect of this process for agriculture has particular relevance for forestry in many countries today. Largely by a trial and error process extending over several generations, farmers everywhere have come to know the productive capacities of their land, to concentrate their energies and their inputs of labor and materials on the better sites. The margin for agriculture and forestry during the past two generations or longer has been primarily the intensive, not the extensive, margin. This does not mean that no lands have been cleared and newly brought into farming, or into forestry, but it does mean that the greatest increases in total output have come from larger yields from established areas, not from new areas. This trend has been particularly marked in forestry in the United States: in the past 60 years, total wood growth in the United States has increased about three and one-half times from essentially the same total forested area.

We think it highly probable that forestry in general, worldwide, for the next several decades will follow a course similar to that of agriculture of the past few generations, in the sense of increased output from the most productive lands, with many of the poorer sites not intensively used or perhaps not used at all.

FORESTS PLAY MANY ROLES IN NATIONAL LIFE

While it has long been recognized that forests play
many roles in national life in addition to providing wood
fiber for many uses, the nonwood outputs of the forest
are coming increasingly to be recognized and valued
everywhere in the world. Forests have watershed values;
while this role of forests has often been exaggerated,
it is a very real one.   Especially in areas with
fragile and easily eroded soils, tree cover may be highly
valuable simply as protection to the watershed. Forests
are the home for many species of wildlife, including
mammals, reptiles, birds, and insects. Some of these
forms of wildlife are clearly valuable to man, others
less obviously so, at least for the present. Ecologists
have been much disturbed at the reduction in wildlife
numbers, sometimes to the point of extinction, as tropical forests are cleared. Forests have a high aesthetic
value for some persons.
Especially in the higher income countries, but to
some extent in all countries, forests are valued as a
place for outdoor recreation. The kinds of forests most
valuable for outdoor recreation are not always the same
as the kinds most valuable for wood production, and vice
versa. The dense forest with trees closely spaced to
take full advantage of the sunlight, moisture, and fertility to grow wood, is often less attractive to the
recreationist than a more open forest. For outdoor recreation, as for wood production, the nearby availability
of a forest to where people live is highly important.
While these nonwood outputs of the forest are valuable, and indeed sometimes far more valuable than the
wood grown, it is wood which is the "paying partner"
in most forests. Under the institutional arrangements
in most countries, including the legal definitions of
property, the owner/manager of the forest is unable to
capture any income from watershed values he may create;
he may be restrained by law from damaging the watershed
but he is unlikely to be rewarded in financial terms for
the water flowing from the forest. The same is true of
wildlife in most countries: in some countries, hunting
rights in the forest can be sold or leased but this provides no protection or incentive for wildlife other than
game species. While the forest owner/manager may have a
full legal right to exclude persons seeking outdoor recreation, often it is very difficult to protect the
forest against trespass. Trespass for wood, or the
unauthorized cutting and removal of wood, is of course
not unknown but is vastly less of a problem than trespass
for other purposes. Since the forest owner/manager
receives no financial return from the production of
forest outputs other than wood, it is not surprising

that investments and expenditures to produce these other outputs are often at a minimum.

Wood grown in forests serves many roles in the economic and social life of a country. Its role as fuel is highly important in many regions, as noted earlier. Wood is essential in the building process everywhere, as scaffolding and forms if nothing else. Wood is incorporated into the structure of most buildings, even those primarily of stone, brick, or clay. Much of the world's furniture is made in whole or in part of wood. Most of the world's paper is made from wood, and one rather reliable index to the degree of economic development of a country is its per capita consumption of paper. As an economy and society develop economically, paper is used as packaging material, in communications, and in scores of other uses. No really satisfactory substitute for paper exists for many of its uses. While computers and electronic communication reduce the need for paper in some roles, they increase the need for it in other roles, and there is no real evidence that the electronic revolution will reduce our dependency upon paper.

Wood, especially in its unprocessed form, is bulky and heavy in relation to its value per unit. Hence local supplies of wood protected from external competitors are valuable. This is especially true in low income countries where transport is limited and relatively expensive. If wood and its products are lacking from local production, some will be "imported" from elsewhere in the same country or from other countries. No country, however low its income per capita, can function without at least some paper, even if this must be imported at high cost.

Wood, no less than any other raw material of high desirability or essentiality, becomes more valuable per unit as it becomes increasingly scarce. In desert and semi-desert areas, for instance, a few poles may be extremely valuable for various forms of construction-- poles of a quality which would be scorned in forest-rich countries. Likewise, where other sources of fuel are very scarce or entirely lacking, wood from small trees and shrubs may have value when such wood would not be used at all in regions or countries blessed with better forest resources. The growing of a few scrawny trees for poles, posts, or fuel in an inhospitable environment may not be a glamorous kind of forestry, appealing to the professional forester, but it may be highly valuable in the economic and social life of the area. In many of the forest-rich countries of the Western Hemisphere, natural forests were so abundant for so many decades that wood was cheap and there was little incentive to invest in growing more wood. Now that wood prices have risen greatly in most of the world, the economic

incentives to grow wood are greater and forest owners/
managers are responding with greater wood production.

BIOLOGICAL AND ECONOMIC CHARACTERISTICS OF FORESTS

Forests have certain biological and economic characteristics which greatly affect the limits within which
national policy on forests may be established. First of
all, tree growth extends over a period of years. For
some species, the major growth period of the tree may be
as little as a dozen years; at the other extreme, for
other species, it may be measured in hundreds of years.
The period from the establishment of the seedling until
the economically optimum harvest date is much shorter
than the total life of the tree, but it still ranges from
half a dozen years to close to a hundred. Trees, like
other biological organisms, go through characteristic
growth stages: birth, childhood, adolescence, young
adulthood, maturity, senescence, and finally death.
There is an age when the maximum total volume of wood
is attained in the individual tree or in a stand of even-
aged trees, from which decline and death take place at
varying older ages. There is an earlier stage of maximum
average annual growth since establishment of the seedling
or the stand; and there is still an earlier stage of most
favorable economic harvest. These are stages on the
growth curve, not invariable points or dates, and they
are all subject to the influence of management programs
for the establishment and care of the tree and the stand.
The classic forestry model contemplates the establishment of a stand at one date, minimal care for the
growth period, and then harvest, followed by another
cycle. In this model, most of the expense comes at the
beginning and all of the income comes at the end. Modern
forestry is different in that more expenses occur during
the growing life of the stand, as more inputs are made,
and in that revenues, sometimes very substantial revenues,
are obtainable during the life of the stand, by thinnings
and from other sources. But, under the most favorable
circumstances, forestry is not something to be picked up
quickly, engaged for a short period, and then abandoned.
Trees, like all biological organisms, and forests,
like all biological communities, have great capacity to
establish themselves and to become re-established after
natural damage or destruction such as fire, storm, disease, or pests, or after harvest. If this were not so,
neither trees nor forests would exist naturally. Once
a seedling has put down its first root, the tree has no
capacity to move; it can only accommodate to its immediate environment or perish. Trees do indeed have
defensive strength against all enemies, but movement to

a more favorable location is not one of them. One should never underestimate the capacity of any natural forest ecosystem to re-establish itself. There have been many instances around the world where forests came back, perhaps not wholly in their original form, after the most violent of disturbances. But neither should anyone assume blithely that every forest ecosystem will become re-established regardless of the shocks it may experience. There are too many illustrations around the world of forest systems not becoming re-established, at least within any reasonable period of human lifetimes. Forest managers, economists, and national policy makers should not assume that the natural forest can be quickly or easily re-established after it is cut or otherwise destroyed.

From an economic point of view, the most outstanding characteristic of forests is the large amount of capital tied up in the growing trees in relation to the annual additions to their volume. A good farm crop involves an annual harvest which returns manyfold the seed planted; the value of the growing crop, at any moment, is small compared with the value of the annual harvest. In the case of forests, a forest which is adding as much as 10 percent annually to the volume of its standing timber is highly productive; many temperate zone forests add substantially less than this. If the trees are large enough to harvest and yield a positive return from the harvest, then an interest return on the capital tied up in the standing trees is often the largest single item of cost of growing more wood in this stand. From the viewpoint of the nonforester, trees may look like the embodiment of natural biological forces working themselves toward a foreordained conclusion. From an economist's viewpoint, forests are highly capital intensive, and the successful growth and harvest of the forest is far from assured. Although forestry is capital intensive in the foregoing sense, it is also true that forestry in many countries and regions provides employment to considerable numbers of people, generally local people and often not highly skilled ones. Thus, under some conditions, forestry lends itself very well to public works employment programs, especially for some operations such as tree planting.

In most economically developed countries there are some environmental groups who oppose the harvest of trees. They argue for preservation of the uncut forest. While some forests might well be preserved uncut for some special purposes such as wilderness or outdoor recreation, if timber is to be grown, and to be utilized, trees must be cut. Everyone can appreciate that cutting cannot indefinitely exceed tree growth, for the inventories are reduced, in the extreme but not unknown case

to zero. It is less generally appreciated that growth
cannot indefinitely exceed harvest, for then inventories
get built up to the maximum that the site will support,
and no more net growth occurs--such growth as there is,
is offset by mortality. Economic forest management involves growing trees and harvesting them. The essential
issues are how much to invest in growing, when and how
to harvest, and how much inventory to maintain.

OWNERSHIP OF FORESTS AND PROCESSING FACILITIES

There are a great many different situations around
the world for the ownership and/or control of the forests, the forestland, and the necessary wood processing
facilities. A few illustrative situations may be discussed briefly.

In a great many countries, some or all of the forestland is owned by government--sometimes by local governments. Where this is true, there is nearly always a
unique history of land ownership which accounts in considerable part for the present forest ownership. But
there is also a widespread feeling in many countries
that governments can take a longer view of forestry than
can or will private owners, with more concern for forest
regeneration and for conservation forest management.
Some of those who hold this view point to the slow growth
rates of many forests and the low rates of return to
capital, which in their view make conservation forestry
most unlikely in private ownership. Some persons will
stress the ability of governments to recognize the nonwood values of forests that are typically not captured
by the forest owner and to manage the forests for both
nonwood and wood values. All of these claims to the
superiority of public management of forests can be, and
have been, challenged, but few observers would deny that
such attitudes are widely held in many countries.

Critics of government forestry can point out that
government forest management may be inefficient in the
sense that it is costly in relation to the values created; or that government forest managers are slow to
respond to changing economic conditions; or that management of the forests is subject to political maneuvering,
with desirable investments often lagging and with specific forest management measures being taken more with an
eye to popular reaction than to silvicultural soundness.
Such critics can find many examples to support their
contentions.

While government ownership and management of the
forestland and the timber stands are common throughout
the world, government ownership and management of the
processing facilities necessary for turning the logs

into lumber, plywood, paper, and other products are much
less common, but far from unknown. In many countries,
the forest is publicly owned; the processing facilities
are privately owned. Under these circumstances, there
is a necessary symbiotic relationship between public and
private activities--and an inevitable rivalry between
them also. Problems inevitably arise in the terms of
timber sale and harvest, the price of the timber, the
length of term for which commitments are made, and other
factors. Although references may be made (in the popular literature especially) to "competitive sale" of
timber from the publicly-owned forests, in fact, such
sales cannot be competitive in the pure economists'
sense of the term. If all the forests are publicly
owned, there is but a single seller; even when some of
the forests are public owned and some are privately
owned, as in the United States, the public forests are
often so large that they dominate the supply side of the
equation. If there is but a single wood processing
plant--sawmill, plywood factory, or paper mill--then
the market is equally defective on the demand side.
This type of situation, of single seller and single
buyer, exists in many economically undeveloped countries
with large natural forest resources; commercial exploitation of those forests depends upon enlistment of a
private processing firm, often a foreign one, and the
negotiation of fair, equitable, and efficient sales
arrangements and prices is difficult indeed. But even
economically more developed countries face somewhat
similar problems in some regions.

At perhaps the other extreme of forest-processing
plant control and operation is the large vertically integrated private forestry firm, which owns its own
forests, has its own processing facilities, neither
buys nor sells timber, and has its own marketing facilities, perhaps reaching into other countries as well.
Vertical integration offers great possibilities for
efficiency in every raw material-handling type of economic enterprise, and forestry is no exception. The
processing plant can be designed to handle the type and
volume of wood which the forests can produce; or the
forest operations can be designed to produce the type
of wood the processing plant is designed to handle; or
there may be some adjustment from each side. Timber
harvest can be scheduled to meet processing plant needs,
and even such matters as seed nursery operations can be
geared to planned timber harvest, including seed selection of strains, species most adapted to replanting on
the sites planned for harvest. Processing plants can be
designed to make the most efficient utilization of the
inevitable by-products from the chief wood processing
operation--chips and sawdust from the sawmill utilized

for paper production, for instance. And to all of these
advantages in wood growing and processing are added the
advantages of a marketing system geared on the one hand
to the supply of materials and on the other hand to the
requirements of the market.

These advantages of vertical integration in forestry,
and the rather large scale of enterprises needed to
achieve these efficiencies are major factors in the
growth of vertical integration in forestry, often by the
merger of smaller firms, which has occurred since World
War II in many countries, including the United States.
Many of the larger vertically integrated forestry firms
have become international in their operations. While
forestry is neither as much in the hands of a few giant
firms nor as wholly international as most oil extraction
and processing, it has moved a long way toward such
large size and international character in the past generation.

One should not, of course, leave the impression that
large vertically integrated forestry firms are neatly
efficient and problem-free. Like any large-scale enterprises, they have their problems of internal organization, efficient management, bureaucratization, and even
lethargy.

In many countries, there is a degree of vertical
integration in forestry firms, but in a less "pure" form
than suggested above. That is, the large firms may both
buy timber from other forest owners and sell timber to
other forest processors. This is governed by differences
in type of quality or size of timber, or by location of
timber supplies in relation to processing facilities, or
by other factors. The firm may have forestlands under
long-term leases or concessions from governments, giving
them some but not all of the management problems and
opportunities that forest ownership would give. The
processing firm might sell some part of its output to
some large-scale marketer. Many other combinations or
degrees of integration may exist, each with its particular circumstances, advantages, and disadvantages.

The United States has about as mixed a forest owner-
ship/forest processing system as any country. There are
large publicly owned forests--nearly 89 million acres in
1977 of commercial forest in the national forests managed by the Forest Service; nearly 11 million acres in
other federal ownership, the management responsibility
divided among several federal agencies; 23 million acres
in State ownership; 7 million acres owned by local governments, mostly counties; 6 million acres owned by
Indian tribes and managed as tribal property; 69 million
acres owned by forest industry firms which operate primary wood processing plants; and 278 million acres privately owned by corporations or individuals which or who

lack such primary processing facilities. Somewhat less
than half of the privately owned forest not having processing facilities was in farms. With rare exceptions,
the publicly owned forests lacked processing facilities
and were dependent upon private processors for sale of
the timber available for harvest.

There are thus a great many different kinds of forest
ownership/forest processing situations in the United
States, especially on a local or regional basis. Because
logs are heavy in relation to value, and because primary
processing often results in a substantial weight loss of
product as compared with raw material, the market for
logs is generally geographically constrained. In some
areas, the Forest Service may be nearly the only seller
of timber. In many areas, there may be but a single
processor for both public and private timber. Under
these circumstances, the local area may face all the
problems of an economically underdeveloped country nego-
tiating with a foreign processing firm. But in other
situations, although there is closely limited competition for timber over much of the area, there may be
competition between firms at the margins of the supply
areas. There are also interesting and sometimes complex
interrelations for the processor between the use of wood
it grows on its forests and the purchase of wood grown
by other owners on their forests.

On the basis of experience in the world to date, one
may tentatively conclude that the advantages of any system of forest ownership or of forest/processing arrangements are not so universal as to dominate the scene.
That is, the fact that many different situations and
arrangements exist somewhere, and sometimes simultaneously in the same region, suggests that each form of
forest ownership has some advantages under some conditions.

Regardless of who owns the forestland and timber and
the forest processing facilities, governments will almost
surely have some role to play in forestry. There is
often the provision of infrastructure of various kinds--
general transportation and communication networks,
general business regulation, general governmental activities such as courts and law enforcement, and the like.
There is often the provision of forestry infrastructure--
activities specialized to forestry, but often of a type
or a scale that individual forest owners cannot well
provide for themselves. Forest fire prevention and control is one such example, as is provision of forest nur-
series to grow seedlings of desired species for planting
by forest owners, especially the smaller ones; insect
and disease control; and especially research on biological, engineering, and economic matters which few if any
private owners can perform for themselves. Governments
may, and often have, provided subsidies to private

forestry actions such as tree planting. The rationale
for such subsidies will be considered later.

ECONOMIC ANALYSIS APPLIED TO FORESTRY

    Economic analysis is fully applicable to forestry.
Forestry presents some unusual and difficult but not insurmountable problems for the economic analyst. What
natural resource does not? There are special problems
because some of the outputs of the forest are generally
not traded in commercial markets, hence it is necessary
to estimate shadow prices for them. There are special
problems because the markets for all forest products,
including wood, are often imperfect in the economist's
sense of the term. Where there is a price for wood, it
may be far from the price that would have arisen from
perfect competition. This imperfect price may mislead
an unwary analyst into treating it as if it were in fact
a competitive price. There are problems of externalities, of costs and values not accruing to the decision-
maker. There are many problems of individual and social
attitudes, not based upon economics and sometimes not
based on any factual foundation, that nevertheless may
greatly affect management decisions. There are especially difficult problems of time dimensions--such as
costs incurred at one time or by one generation, values
obtained at another time or by another generation.
One could add to this list other problems which the economic analyst must face in forestry.
    Some foresters and some other persons believe that
forests are "good" in some absolute sense, almost irre-
spective of costs and tangible benefits. In contrast,
we believe that forests are often valuable natural
resources, capable of use to individual and group economic and social benefit, but we reject any assertion
that forests are somehow above economic considerations.
We assert that forestry should be and can be subjected
to economic analysis as well as any other resource-based
human activity. This philosophical or conceptual convic-
tion underlies our own considerable research activity on
forestry.
    One major economic consideration (but not the only
one) is economic efficiency in foresty: how do the costs
compare with the benefits? Clearly, there are often
uncertainties about both costs and benefits, the latter
in particular both because they may come at some relatively distant future date and because the benefit
values often are not captured in a market price. But
the uncertainties exist whether economic analysis is
made or not; a careful analysis may help to define the
uncertainty and to put it in perspective. Economic

analysis can be applied to publicly and privately owned
forests. Public resources or funds are not costless in
either a financial or economic sense; public funds used
for forestry clearly cannot be used for other activities,
public or private. The outputs of publicly owned forests
are not cost-free.

It has become generally recognized in recent years
that economic analysis can profitably be employed in consideration of highway or other transportation networks,
in education, in health, and elsewhere in the traditional
public service. This is not, of course, to assert that
all public decisions on such activities have been guided
or controlled by economic considerations. But there is
an increasing public awareness that the costs should be
estimated and, as far as possible, compared with the
gains expected. The fact that some costs and many benefits do not find regular monetary expression does not
make them any less real. The same concepts are gradually
being extended to forestry. In the United States, the
past decade has seen at least two major laws, one major
thrust of which was to extend to public forest management
the concepts of economic efficiency--expressed in non-
economic terms in the laws, but nonetheless of clear
intent.

Economic efficiency as applied to forests clearly
should be for the whole forest cycle or longer, not
merely for the harvest of existing stands. The latter
indeed may be subjected to economic analysis as part of
a more extended cycle. The economic analysis must include the necessary infrastructure or ancillary facilities such as transportation, communication, water supply,
waste disposal, and others.

Economic analysis as applied to forestry must consider the costs borne and the advantages gained by the
decision-maker, private or public. In many cases, the
private owner/manager/exploiter of forest resources
neither bears all the costs nor gains all the benefits
from his decisions and actions. We have noted how watershed and wildlife values, to name but two, generally do
not accrue to the forest owner. The national economy
will--must--bear all the costs and will gain all the
values, and thus the national planner must consider a
wider range of both costs and benefits than is rational
for the private forest owner to consider. But this most
certainly does not mean that the public benefits are
limitless nor that they are costless, nor that economic
efficiency is not as important here as for the private
costs and benefits.

While the national planner should consider all the
costs and all the benefits from any forestry program in
the country, economic analysis should not stop merely at
calculation of benefits and cost efficiency; instead, it

should also include considerations of incidence of both
costs and benefits--who pays, and who gains? In forestry
there is often a substantial disassociation of costs and
benefits. One group--often the general taxpayer--bears
the costs, while the benefits often accrue to a smaller
though perhaps ill-defined group. We do not argue that
costs and benefits should always be shared exactly in
the same proportions--that would be a standard that would
render much resource use impossible; but we do argue that
the incidence of costs and benefits should be estimated
as accurately as possible, so that legislative bodies and
officials at least know the distributional effects of
their programs. We would further argue that, to the extent operationally practical, costs and benefits should
be brought into at least approximate balance. We think
the quality of the public decision making process would
be greatly improved if this were done.

Economics should be applied to the productive process
of wood growing. Many foresters in many countries propose to make their decisions about timber growing and
timber harvest on "silvicultural grounds," which in practice often means the growing of relatively very large
trees, often at slow growth rates in order to have the
dense wood that results from narrow annual growth rings,
and often under a relatively extensive system of forest
management. Public foresters in the past have generally
not been called upon to justify in economic terms their
forest management practices, but, as noted earlier, this
may be changing. As private forestry has gotten more
and more into large-scale and highly commercial enterprises, forest management has come to be influenced by
standards of efficiency of production. The economist
who analyzes forestry as an economic enterprise is highly
dependent upon the ecologists, the silviculturalists,
the forest mensurationists, and other biological, physical, and engineering specialists. But he would also be
wise to insist upon evidence and upon quantitative data
as to biological relationships, and to make his own
analysis based upon such data, rather than accept at
face value the management recommendations of the foresters. In this regard, of course, forestry is not
really unique--the same thing is true of water development or of agriculture. The production specialist is
invaluable but not infallible in making management
recommendations.

As forestry enters the intensive stage, with more
production inputs and a greater range of them, economic
analysis becomes doubly important. The alternatives
increase, and deciding on choices among alternatives is
where economics often has a great deal to offer.

PRODUCTION AND INTERNATIONAL TRADE

The world's forestry resources are broadly distributed (table 1). As measured in either land area or growing stock (timber inventory), the USSR (with 33 percent
of the world's volume) is the dominant region. However,
North America (with 16 percent of the growing stock),
South America (with 27 percent), and Asia (with 15 percent) also have large portions of the world's total
forest resources, while Europe's portion is relatively
modest (5 percent). Africa and Oceania make up the remainder. The world conifer (softwood) forests are less
evenly distributed, with the USSR and North America
accounting for about 85 percent of the world's total;
adding Europe brings the percentage to over 90 percent.
Broadleaf (hardwood) forests are perhaps somewhat more
evenly distributed, with South America and Asia accounting for over 70 percent by volume and the USSR and North
America accounting for another 18 percent. While South
America has about 34 percent of the total land area and
about 50 percent of the total global volume of broadleaf
forests, it has less than 1 percent of the total area and
volume of the world's coniferous forests.

In 1976 the traditional world timber producers--North
America, Europe, and the USSR--accounted for 46 percent
of the world's roundwood (unprocessed harvested wood) production. However, their dominance in 1976 was greater for
industrial roundwood (76 percent) and still greater for
conifer industrial roundwood (88 percent). This dominance,
as reflected in the share of worldwide production, eroded
considerably since 1959, the earliest date for which data
are available. In 1959 the traditional producers' shares
were 66 percent, 83 percent, and 92 percent for roundwood, industrial roundwood, and conifer industrial roundwood, respectively. The decline in the dominance of the
traditional producers, of course, reflects the growth in
production by the other regions of the world.

It is also revealing to examine net intercontinental
forest product trade flows, i.e., the net trade flows by
value between the seven world "continents"--North America
(the United States and Canada), Latin America, Europe,
Africa, Asia, the USSR and Oceania. In 1967 three conti-
nents--North America, the USSR, and Africa--had net forest
product exports with North America accounting for about
two-thirds, the USSR for about one-third, and Africa a
very small portion of net exports. By 1976 Africa had
become a net importer, North America now accounted for
three-fourths and the USSR for one-fourth of the total
net flow. For both of these years, Latin America was a
net importer. However, both the Latin American and
Oceanian fractions of the world's total net imports fell
as these regions moved toward relatively greater self-
sufficiency in forest production.

TABLE 3.1
World Growing Stock: Volume in Closed Forest

Region	Coniferous 100 million cum[b]	%	Broadleaf 100 million cum[b]	%	Combined coniferous & broadleaf forests[a] 100 million cum[b]	%
North America	265	25.8	95	7.8	360	16.1
Central America	7	0.7	15	1.2	22	1.0
South America	5	0.5	595	49.1	600	26.8
Africa	1	0.1	51	4.2	52	2.3
Europe	80	7.8	40	3.3	120	5.4
USSR	612	59.5	120	9.9	733	32.7
Asia	55	5.3	285	23.5	340	15.2
Oceania	3	0.3	10	0.8	13	0.5
Total world	1028	100.0	1211	100.0	2240	100.0

Source: Reidar Persson, World Forest Resources: Review of the World's Forest Resources in the Early 1970s (Stockholm, Royal College of Forestry) no. 17 (1974).

[a] Sum of coniferous and broadleaf forests does not always add to total.

[b] cubic meters.

A more disaggregated look at the world reveals only a few regions that are net forest products exporters on a truly large scale. These are the Pacific Northwest region of North America (including British Columbia in Canada) that provides forest products to most major world markets; the East Indian Archipelago of Southeast Asia which includes Indonesia, Malaysia, and the Philippines and provides tropical hardwoods to major world markets; the Nordic countries which provide forest products largely to the United Kingdom and continental Europe; and the much more modest flow of exported logs from the Eastern USSR to Japan.

All of these major flows except that of the Nordic countries represent the utilization of a large timber resource that was the bequest of nature. The Nordic case represents the outgrowth of conscious investments in plantation forests utilizing indigenous species.

Analogous to the principal producing regions, we can identify three dominant forest product consuming regions: Continental Europe (including the United Kingdom), the Northeast and North Central regions of the United States, and Japan. Continental European forest products are supplied by local sources, with the dominating external flow coming from the Nordic countries. In addition, Canada, the United States (both the Pacific Northwest and the South), and the USSR provide forest products. Finally, smaller flows to Europe originate in Latin America, Africa, and Southeast Asia.

The Northeast and the North Central regions of the United States are supplied largely from the U.S. South and Canada (both eastern and western). Additional inflows originate in the Pacific Northwest. Finally, Japan draws broadly throughout the Pacific Basin for her forest products.

While there was not a dramatic improvement in Latin America's overall forest products trade between 1967 and 1976, some positive signs were noted (see table 2). Both exports and imports in 1976 were a smaller share of total forest products trade than in 1967 and the decline in the import share was somewhat larger as the rate of growth of exports exceeded the rate of growth of imports. Also, the Latin American share of the intercontinental forest products deficit declined. Moreover, fragmentary evidence suggests that in very recent years the situation has improved markedly. This appears to be particularly true for certain commodities. For example, table 3 shows a remarkable increase in the production of both pulp and paper and paperboard. The dramatic increase in Latin America's share of the value of world total production attests to the relative pace of that increase. Tables 4 and 5 show the six largest Latin American producer countries in 1979. The point here

TABLE 3.2
Latin American Forest Products Trade
(millions of current U.S. $)

	1961-65 average	1976
Total Latin American exports	$ 96.9	$ 476.1
Percentage of world total	1.5%	1.2%
Total Latin American imports	343.4	1,128.2
Percentage of world total	4.5%	3.2%
Net intercontinental deficit as percentage of world total	16.0%	8.4%

Source: Postwar Trends in U.S. Forest Products Trade, by
Roger A. Sedjo and Samuel J. Radcliffe. Research Paper
No. 22, Resources for the Future, Washington, D.C. (1981).

TABLE 3.3
Pulp Production and Paper and Paperboard Production
(000 metric tons)

Pulp

	1960	1970	1979
Latin America	821	2,224	4,761
World total	60,031	107,157	128,939
Latin America as Per- cent of world total	1.37	2.08	3.68

Paper and Paperboard

	1960	1970	1979
Latin America	1,656	3,712	7,269
World total	74,355	129,298	171,015
Latin America as Per- cent of world total	2.22	2.87	4.25

Source: Paper and Pulp (August, 1980) p. 64.

TABLE   3.4
Major Pulp Producers in Latin America

Country	Percent of total Latin American value of production 1979
Brazil	51
Mexico	15
Chile	15
Argentina	9
Colombia	4
Peru	2

Source: Paper and Pulp (August 1980) p. 64.

TABLE   3.5
Major Paper and Paperboard Producers in Latin America

Country	Percent of total Latin American value of production 1979
Brazil	41
Mexico	36
Argentina	17
Venezuela	11
Colombia	5
Chile	4

Source: Paper and Pulp (August 1980) p. 64.

is that Latin American production of certain forest products is growing considerably faster than is world production.

WORLDWIDE TRANSITION FROM NATURAL TO PLANTATION FORESTS

One of the most exciting features of contemporary forestry is the increasing role that industrial plantation forests--forests planned, managed, and harvested for their industrial wood values--are playing in meeting the world's growing wood requirements. Historically, man has met his needs for wood by utilizing the natural forest in a manner akin to the hunting and foraging mode employed by early man to meet his food and fiber needs. The initial endowments of forest resources were far in excess of early man's wood requirements, and made concern about the resource unwarranted. As with hunting and foraging resources, timber resources were largely treated as a common property resource with the significant expense of wood products being related to harvest, transport, and processing costs. Through time, of course, hunting and foraging have been almost entirely replaced by livestock raising and agriculture. Similarly, the world is currently experiencing a transition from reliance upon natural unmanaged forests to an increasing reliance upon managed plantation forests to provide a larger share of the world's wood needs.

The transition from natural to plantation forests has, thus far, been very gradual. Typically, plantations have been established to replace the harvested natural forest. This is particularly true in regions such as Europe and much of North America, where the process of natural regeneration is increasingly being displaced by artificial regeneration.

In the tropics and the Southern Hemisphere, the introduction of industrial forest plantations has proceeded slowly. True, before World War II some countries developed rather large forest plantations. Industrial plantations were established in New Zealand, South Africa, and Chile as well as parts of Asia and Africa. In Brazil, around the turn of the century, fast-growing eucalyptus plantations were developed to provide fuel for the railroad systems. But on a global scale these activities were quite modest indeed.

After World War II, and particularly after 1960, the tempo of forest plantation development increased dramatically in regions of the tropics and Southern Hemisphere. The preliminary successes of many of these plantations, the rapid biological growth rates often achieved, and the vast land areas potentially available suggest the

long-term possibility for meeting much of the world's increasing wood and wood fiber requirement with expanded
production from the forest plantations of the tropics
and the Southern Hemisphere.
          Three major plantation types can be charac-
terized as occurring currently across the world. First,
in temperate regions that traditionally produced the
majority of the world's industrial wood--Northern Europe
and North America--plantations utilizing indigenous species have typically replaced cutover natural forests.
Second, other temperate regions that have not traditionally been major industrial wood producers are commonly
introducing exotic temperate climate species (largely
North American) in their plantations--species that exhibit rapid growth and desired merchantibility. Third,
certain tropical regions are introducing exotic species
(tropical pines, eucalyptus, gmelina) from other tropical regions which exhibit desirable growth and merchant-
ability characteristics. While experience with exotic
plantations in the tropics is limited, results thus far
are so dramatic that some knowledgeable observers have
concluded that tropical regions will eventually become
dominant wood suppliers.
     Although plantations are presently a small fraction
of the world's total forested area, the land areas involved belie their true potential. Industrial potential
is the result of not only more land being converted into
forest plantations, but also of the volume of output per
land unit. These volumes are likely to be large for
plantations since the location is usually determined by
considerations of high biological growth and because
management practices usually associated with plantations
increase usable growth. Plantations do not merely plant
trees, but almost always include other intensive management practices. Thus, fast-growing forest plantations
offer the potential of meeting a major share of the
world's timber supply requirements from relatively small
areas of forest plantation.

SOME EXAMPLES OF INDUSTRIAL PLANTATION EXPERIENCE

     Outside of Europe and North America, only a few re-
gions have developed large industrial plantation forests.
New Zealand currently has about one million hectares in
plantation forests, most of it in exotic conifer from
North America. New Zealand is adding to these forests
at a rate of some 50,000 hectares per year and has become a factor in Pacific Basin markets. Australia has
also introduced exotic plantations, particularly conifers, to provide for her domestic long fiber requirements. Industrial plantation forestry of various types

is underway in the Philippines, Indonesia and Malaysia,
and India. Japan has some 10 million hectares of plantation forest, although not all of it is industrial
plantation. Numerous parts of Africa have also been
involved in various forestry schemes. Industrial plantations have been created in Kenya and Tanzania in East
Africa, utilizing a variety of tropical conifer species.
South Africa has undertaken large plantations of various
species. West Africa has been involved in plantation
schemes utilizing eucalyptus, gmelina, and tropical
pines.

Of all the nontraditional producing areas of the
globe, however, industrial forest plantations appear to
have the greatest potential in South America. Plantations have been in place in Chile for about seventy-five
years, and Chile currently has about 700,000 hectares of
plantation forests. In recent years the planting activity in Chile has increased to almost 80,000 hectares
per year and Chile has begun to actively enter world
markets within recent years. Significant plantation
activity is also underway in Colombia and Argentina. In
Venezuela, serious interest in large industrial plantations has developed only within the past decade or less.
However, the level of activity is substantial, involving
hundreds of thousands of hectares, and appears to have
great potential, due to the availability of large areas
of land with few alternative uses and a location astride
a major navigable artery which provides access to the
sea. The country of greatest potential, however, is
probably Brazil. This expectation springs from the fact
that biological growth rates in Brazil are very rapid
compared with those experienced in North America. The
land areas of Brazil that are available for forest plantations are vast and in many cases the opportunity costs
of the land are quite small. Brazil's location vis-à-vis
major world markets is quite favorable. Since the mid-
1960s Brazil has established over 3 million hectares of
fast-growing industrial forest plantations from the tropical Amazon to the temperate climate regions of the South.

GLOBAL TRENDS IN FOREST PLANTATIONS

A recent FAO study provides some perspective on the
global extent of forest plantations. As table 6 shows,
all areas regenerated by artificial means totaled 90
million hectares in the mid-1970s. A large part of these
plantations were located in the traditional producing
temperate climate regions of Europe, North America and
the USSR. Also, China had some 30 to 40 million hectares
of plantation forest and South Korea added about 4 million

TABLE 3.6
Man-made Forests, mid-1970s

Economic class and region	Million hectares
Developed	
North America	11
Western Europe	13
Oceania	1
Other	10
Total	35
Developing	
Africa	2
Latin America	3
Asia	3
Total	8
Centrally planned	
Europe and the Soviet Union	17
Asia	30
Total	47
Total world	90

Source: Food and Agricultural Organization of the United Nations. Development and investment in the forestry sector. FAO:COFO-78/2. (Rome, 1978) 21 pp.

hectares. Of course, not all of the world's 90 million hectares are industrial plantations. For example, many of the forests in China are designed primarily for protection and/or fuelwood with only limited attention given to industrial potential.

Man-made forests compose roughly 3 percent of the closed forest area and include all areas regenerated by artificial means including conventional afforestation and deforestation techniques. Conifers are generally the preferred species for industrial plantations, although large areas of eucalyptus and gmelina have been established in Latin America, particularly in Brazil.

While the majority of forest plantations are situated in the Northern Hemisphere temperate climate regions, in recent years increased attention has been given to plantation activities in the tropics and subtropics, and in the Southern Hemisphere temperate climate regions. Table 7 summarizes a study of forest plantations in the tropics. The study estimated that the tropic and subtropic regions of Central and South America, Africa and Asia had about 11.8 million hectares of plantation forest in the mid-1970s. Of this, about 6.7 million hectares were industrial forest plantations.

By 1980, a period of only five years later, the industrial forest plantations were projected by FAO to increase by 36 percent to 9.1 million hectares, and projections for the year 2000 indicated the industrial plantations in that region would reach over 21 million hectares. Although these figures include slow-growing specialty woods such as teak, the majority of the present and projected tropic and subtropical industrial plantations consist of fast-growing conifers and hardwoods designated for ordinary solid wood and fiber production.

POTENTIAL IMPACT OF PLANTATIONS UPON WORLD PRODUCTION AND TRADE

The long-term supply of forest resources has been a topic of concern for some years. In the United States the concern has been expressed in terms of the adequacy of domestic supply. Internationally, the FAO has expressed concern over the long-run adequacy of world supply. Recently, the recognition has been growing that the tropical regions have substantial potential to supplement worldwide production of industrial wood and particularly the coniferous wood that is in relatively short supply.

The implications of economically viable commercial forest plantations could be quite profound. As the natural forests of the world are increasingly utilized,

TABLE 3.7
Industrial Plantations--Tropical and Subtropical
America, Africa and Asia

	1975	Projected 1980	Projected 2000
Central and South America	2,786	4,128	10,705
Africa south of Sahara[a]	997	1,248	2,180
Developing Asia[b] and the Far East	2,892	3,719	8,265
Total	6,675	9,095	21,150

Source: J. P. Lanly and J. Clement. "Present and Future
Natural Forest and Plantation Areas in the Tropics,"
Unasylva vol 13, no. 123 (1979) pp. 12-20.

[a]excluding South Africa

[b]From Pakistan east excluding the Peoples Republic of
China, Mongolia, and Japan.

the residual unharvested natural forest will become increasingly inaccessable. Although the technology of man-made forests has long been available, the economics of commercial forest plantation investments in many regions of the world has been questionable. Recent evidence, however, suggests that the economics of plantation forests is steadily becoming more favorable. This evidence is of three types. First, the market test reveals that private forest plantation investments are increasingly being made in a number of different locations throughout the world. In addition, project evaluation studies which examine the economic returns to forestry in various regions around the globe, including a global study undertaken at Resources for the Future, also suggest competitive returns from forest investments. Still, such a finding ought not to be surprising to those familiar with resource price behavior. In a study done at RFF in the late 1950s, Potter and Christy found that wood primary products were one of the few natural resources that had been experiencing an increase in real prices over the previous seventy-five years. In a recent update of this study, Manthy found that the trend of increasing real prices for wood had continued into the early 1970s.

These considerations provide prima facie evidence of the growing economic scarcity of certain types of wood, increasing the economic incentive to invest in its production. The implication of commercial forest plantations that are economically viable could be quite profound. Over the years, a concern has been expressed that there is a growing scarcity of timber. In the United States this concern has been expressed periodically in the pronoucements of various committees and in the projections of the Forest Service. Globally, international organizations, such as the Food and Agricultural Organization of the United Nations, have expressed concern over the long-run adequacy of the world's wood supply both for forest product production and for use as fuel.

In addition to concerns over the adequacy of the world's wood supply are concerns expressed over the rate at which the tropical forests of the world are being eliminated. While this is far too large and complex an issue to be addressed in this paper, it should be noted that most of the destruction of the world's tropical forests is not due to commercial logging but is due to other factors, e.g. slash and burn agriculture. Commercial logging of these forests is a factor in certain regions. The creation of economic plantation forests offers promise of providing both a substitute for the wood provided currently by the world's natural forests, and also of generating less ecological damage than would occur if nonforest uses of the land were pursued.

Finally, plantation forests allow forestry investments to be made in regions of the world that have not
had important natural commercial forests. The rapid biological growth of the tropics and Southern Hemisphere are
suggestive of potential high economic returns to forestry
plantation investments. Of course, high biological
growth rates are not the only relevant economic consideration. The opportunity costs of the land, the costs of
plantation establishment, the costs of harvesting and
local transportaiton, the type and quality of stumpage,
processing costs, and transportation costs of the primary
or intermediate product to the market are also important
factors.

RECENT RESEARCH ON ECONOMIC RETURNS TO FOREST PLANTATIONS

Resources for the Future recently undertook a study
of the comparative economics of plantation forestry in
twelve regions of the world. The regions to be examined
were chosen either because they have large-scale plantation activities or because there was reason to believe
that they had substantial economic potential based upon
considerations of biological growth rates, wood quality,
and location vis-à-vis world markets. In each case the
analysis was based upon the country's ability to export
to major world markets--Japan, the Eastern United States,
and Northern Europe. Of the twelve regions selected,
four were in Latin America. There were three in Brazil--
Amazonia, Central Brazil, and Southern Brazil--and Chile
was also included.
An important component of the economic viability of
a forest plantation is the biological yields attainable.
Of course, as with agriculture, yields are dependent on
nature, e.g. soils, climate, and other natural features
peculiar to the site, and also dependent upon discretion-
ary inputs and silvicultural practices, e.g. modes of
planting, seed stock, fertilization, extent of weeding,
thinning, pruning, prescription burning and the like.
Also, as with agriculture, financial returns from plantation forestry depend upon the relation between costs and
income. For our study we assumed a silvicultural regime
that was believed to be approximately economic, i.e., one
that maximized the discounted present value of the forests. In addition, the proximity to world markets and
the cost associated with international transport were
considered as well as wood type and quality as reflected
in species, by size, age, and so forth. Extensive sensi-
tivity analysis was undertaken to identify the assumptions

and data inputs to which the final results were most
sensitive.

The preliminary results suggest that the economics
of forest plantations in Brazil and Chile appear quite
favorable for the production of both pulpwood and
sawtimber. Our results suggest that each of the three
Brazilian regions has favorable inherent wood-growing
economics if the plantation development costs incurred
prior to the establishment of the plantings (including
requisite infrastructure) can be controlled and if the
land's highest value use is forestry. While in the
Chilean case the results are not quite as favorable as
those of Brazil, the Chilean economic returns are quite
comparable with those of most of the better performing
world regions and markedly superior to the economic
returns expected in some of the world's major forest
plantation regions, e.g. the Pacific Northwest of North
America and the Nordic region.

As an example, Chilean forest plantations are blessed
with rapid biological growth and relatively short harvest
rotations. A major weakness of Chilean plantations is
the long distances to the major world markets and the
attendant high international transport costs.

MULTIPLE USE FORESTRY

Much is made in many countries of the idea of multiple use management of both public and private forests.
Undeniably, all forests produce some wood, water, wildlife and scenery; and they may be used to provide
industrial wood, fuelwood, and outdoor recreation,
including often hunting and fishing, and "wilderness"
or a relatively primitive type of outdoor recreation.
In this regard, forests are a classic case of multi-
product firms. Each of the possible outputs of a forest
requires some inputs of land, labor, capital, and management. Each of the various kinds of forest outputs
responds to the amount, kind, and quality of the inputs,
although the degree and nature of that response varies
considerably from one kind of output to another. Neither
the inputs nor the outputs need be in fixed proportions:
some variations are possible. There are trade-offs
between one kind of input and another and between one
kind of output and another. Each kind of output has
value,although these may not be reflected in a market
price. The value per unit of output depends in some
degree upon the volume of such output--more output
nearly always means a lesser value for the marginal
unit, but by varying degrees.

From an economic viewpoint, the test of efficiency
in multiple use management is to substitute one input
for another, or one output for another, until that combination of inputs and outputs is achieved which yields
the highest net present value. One input is substituted
for another, or one output chosen in preference to
another, as long as any adjustment or change increases
the net return of the package. It is not necessary to
arrive at a cost allocation of inputs to outputs in
order to achieve this optimum economic output.

This type of analysis can be made for those costs
which the forest owner/manager bears and those returns
which he obtains, or it can be made in terms of the
whole costs and whole returns regardless of who pays
or who gains. The former costs and returns are typically only a part of the whole, differing between the
different kinds of forest outputs. Thus, as noted
earlier, the forest owner/manager is normally able to
get all or at least a high proportion of the values
created by wood growing and harvest, whereas he gets
little or none of the values created by good watershed
or wildlife management. The owner/manager naturally
takes into account only those costs he bears and those
values he gains, and adjusts his forest management plan
accordingly. Not infrequently, he is constrained by
governmental or social restraints of various kinds--laws
governing the manner of timber harvest to protect watershed values, or local customs about the rights of people
to harvest windfalls, and others. Such laws or social
customs may, or may not, compensate for the lack of
marketability of some of the forest outputs.

There are substantial difficulties in the actual
application of multiple use forest management, but the
theoretical problems are by no means insurmountable.

NATIONAL FOREST POLICY

Forests are too important a natural resource in most
countries to be neglected in any national natural resource planning. The way forests should be used depends
upon the natural endowment of the country for forestry,
upon the stage of economic development of the country,
and upon national goals and aspirations, as noted at the
beginning of this paper. There we also noted some of
the major kinds of forest situations in the world today.
Clearly, different policies and actions by government
are most appropriate, depending upon these conditions
and situations. Nevertheless, there are some common
principles which should underlie national forest policy
in every country.

1. Wise forest policy for the long pull in every
country requires an accurate appraisal of the biological-
physical feasibility and consequences of every proposed
forest management program. There is nothing to be gained
and much may be lost by attempting a forest management
program which in fact is simply not feasible, or in ignoring the likely biological consequences of the proposed
program. If the proposal is to harvest natural forest
stands in humid tropics, how much and what kinds of natural reproduction are likely? If the proposal is to
plant exotic or imported tree species in some location,
what will be the growth rates, what are the likely enemies of the trees or problems in the longer run, what
about re-establishment of tree stand after the first
harvest, and so on? Many such questions must be raised
in every forest situation. The answers to these questions are often uncertain and capable of full resolution
only after many years experience. <u>This surely points to
the wisdom of adequate research and careful monitoring of
the results of every program</u>. It also suggests strongly
that programs should not be undertaken on a large scale
until at least tentative answers to such questions are in
hand.

2. Whatever forest policy or forest management program a country undertakes, it should be prepared to stay
with that policy and program for a considerable number of
years. As noted earlier, forestry is not something that
can be picked up this year, dropped next year, and picked
up in some future year, with any kind of acceptable results. The actual results on the ground come slowly,
sometimes only after more than one cycle of planting and
harvesting, in time spans likely to be measured in decades rather than in years. This does not mean, of course,
that forest policies should not be re-examined critically
at intervals, and perhaps changed after demonstrated
failures or inadequacies. But changes, if any, should be
carefully researched and planned, not matters of passing
whims. This general advice takes different forms in different countries, depending in part upon governmental
procedures. But some form of continuity of policy is essential.

3. Subject to these constraints, every country would
be well advised to develop and use its forest resources
to their maximum economic potential, including the use of
potential forestlands not now in tree cover. Land for
which the growing of economic forests is the highest
value use can be a major national asset, and should be
utilized to the economic optimum. This includes countries with scant forests but where wood is essential as
fuel; it includes countries with substantial capacity to
produce industrial wood for domestic use or for export;
and it includes nonwood forest outputs as well as wood.
As noted earlier, the forest management plans should in-

clude the mixture of forest outputs which maximizes net economic value to the country. The actual programs may, of course, fall short of the ideal for forests, as they often do for programs for other natural resource use and management.

4. An indispensable part of national forest policy must include timber harvest on forests planned for such harvest. Any country may choose to have, or to keep, some forests in park or other nonharvest status, and we do not mean to preclude such forest management. But, if wood production is one of the planned outputs of the forest, then timber harvest is essential. In some countries, there has been substantial opposition by some groups to timber harvest. If a country is not prepared actually to harvest the timber planned for harvest, and for which investments and outlays have been made, then it had best not make such investments or undertake such forest management in the first place.

5. Whether the forests are publicly or privately owned and regardless of the mix of outputs planned from the forest, some degree and kind of government action will be needed if forests are to make their maximum contribution to national welfare. The governmental actions may be no more than provision of general infrastructure, such as roads, or it may be direct government action in management of publicly owned forests. In many countries, there has been considerable subsidization of either public or private forestry or both as economic enterprises. We think subsidies for forestry should be examined most critically; we see nothing unique about forestry which justifies different standards for it than for other aspects of the national economy. As economists, we are naturally skeptical about all subsidies, but we recognize that they exist in many countries. We think that, at a minimum, sharp questions should be asked about objectives, costs, returns, who gains and who pays, and the like, for every proposed forest subsidy program.

The overall outlook for forestry is bright, with many difficult problems and many interesting opportunities.

4
Agricultural Research Policy in Small Developing Countries

D. Gale Johnson

INTRODUCTION

Significant governmental support of agricultural research has a history of less than a century and a half. The preeminence of British agriculture in the 18th and 19th centuries was based, at least in part, on research undertaken by private individuals, usually on their own farms or estates. The famous Rothamsted Experimental Station was established in 1843 by a private institution and remained as such throughout the remainder of the 19th century. The first of the German publicly supported agricultural experimental stations was established almost a decade later in 1852 in Saxony.

Ruttan and Hayami make the following comparison between the development and progress of agricultural research during the last half of the 19th century:[1]

> Although the German system of agricultural research
> evolved later than the British, it provided a more
> effective environment for the "enlargement" of new
> scientific and technical knowledge. As a special-
> ized institution, operating under its own charter
> and supported by the state, it was not as subject
> to the pressures for immediate practical results
> as the privately supported research of the English
> landowners or even the co-operatively organized
> Edinburgh Laboratory. The development of publicly
> supported agricultural research institutions was
> based on the establishment, in Germany, of a social
> and political climate which regarded science and
> technology as instruments of economic growth and
> which viewed their advance as a major responsibility
> of the state.

The Edinburgh Laboratory was founded in 1842 by a voluntary agricultural society in Scotland. According to Ruttan and Hayami:[2] "The laboratory was dissolved in 1848 due to the association members' hastiness in their demand for practical results."

Over time and in most countries publicly supported agricultural research has largely displaced privately supported agricultural research. Except for the United States and Canada, relatively little agricultural research is undertaken by the private sector. It is perhaps not too surprising that this is the case since it is difficult for the private sector to use its own resources in competition with public institutions that rely upon governmental support. But there may be more to this substitution of public for private support than this simple presumption implies.

APPLIED AND BASIC RESEARCH

It is rather commonplace to differentiate between two broad categories of research--basic and applied. My late distinguished colleague, Harry G. Johnson, deftly and accurately defined these two categories of research as follows:[3] "Conceptually, then, basic research is concerned with adding to the stock of human knowledge, whereas applied research is concerned with turning the stock of human knowledge to practical use."

While there are limitations to attempting to make too much of the distinction between basic and applied research with respect to the appropriate sources and degree of support, it is worth pursuing some of the differences between the two types of research. In theory, and to a considerable degree in practice, it is possible to measure the social benefits that result from applied research. In fact, it may be possible to anticipate with some degree of accuracy what benefit will be derived from a particular level of investment in a program of applied research. However, a program of basic research is much less susceptible to any anticipation of the benefits that may result. Whatever benefits may be derived from basic research are likely to come only after a lengthy gestation period. For example, most of the basic genetic research that resulted in the production of hybrid corn was done in the last decade of the Nineteenth Century. However, hybrid corn did not become commercially available until more than a quarter century later. There can be no doubt of the enormous social benefit that was derived from the basic research that made possible the development of hybrid corn as well as the hybridization of numerous other economic crops. The benefits continue and presumably will so long as man depends upon crops for a significant fraction of his food supply.

But one does not want to push this distinction between basic and applied research too far. While it may
be more difficult to estimate the potential benefit from
a given stream of basic science investments than the potential benefit from investments in applied projects, it
does not mean that ex post estimation of the returns from
basic science is impossible or especially difficult.
Robert Evenson has shown that it is possible to derive
estimates of the ex post benefits from the "more basic"
spectrum of agricultural research in much the same way as
the benefits of the "more applied" agricultural research
has been estimated. I will present some of his estimates
later.

Much is often made of the distinction between basic
and applied research in terms of who derives the benefits
resulting from the research. The benefits from basic research are presumed to be wholly social benefits; the
provider of the research captures a nil part of the benefits. Moreover, the benefits from applied research are
often assumed to accrue primarily to whoever does the research. But too much can be made of this distinction,
especially if the distinction is used as a basis for determining who should pay for agricultural research.

It is true that one can imagine a spectrum going
from very basic to highly applied research; at the basic
end of that continuum, the research results benefit society generally while at the very applied end of the continuum the researcher or inventor may derive essentially
all of the benefit. But very little agricultural research is undertaken for which nearly all of the benefits
can be retained by those who undertake or finance the research.

The results of much applied agricultural research
become generally available rather soon. This is true of
the development of new plant varieties, such as the high
yielding varieties of rice and wheat developed during the
1950s and 1960s. A new cultural practice, such as fallow,
minimum tillage, improvements in sanitation or drip irrigation, promptly becomes a public good. This is not to
say that there are no examples of applied research where
the benefits are largely captured by the supporter of
that research--many chemical products used as herbicides
or insecticides or for the prevention of diseases in
plants and animals have resulted from profitable privately financed research. But it cannot be assumed without
investigating each case that the benefits from very applied agricultural research will be retained by the provider of that research.

Even if there is relatively little agricultural research for which the research organization retains all of
the benefits, there is a significant amount of research
for which enough of the benefits are retained to induce
private for-profit organizations to undertake such re-

search. In the United States it is estimated that more
than a quarter of all agricultural research is undertaken
in the private industrial sector; some estimates put the
amount undertaken by the industrial sector at about the
same level as the sum of state and federal direct support
of agricultural research.[4] Thus it must be true that the
private rate of return on research undertaken by the industrial sector is high enough to induce investment in
that research even if part of the benefits are broadly
diffused among other private firms, early adopters, and
consumers generally.

While not too much should be made of it, an implication of the existence of a difference between the social
and private return on privately financed research is that
too little is invested in the research undertaken in the
private sector. In other words, there is a "free rider"
problem that results in some misallocation of resources.
The "free riders" are those that obtain the benefits of
the private research without having to pay for that research. But as is indicated below, the "free rider" problem exists for publicly financed research as well. Publicly financed research is almost wholly financed by individual governments and since a part of the benefits are
realized by individuals and groups living in other countries, a part of the social benefits from agricultural
research may not influence the decisions about investment
in research.

COMPONENTS OF AGRICULTURAL RESEARCH POLICY

A nation's agricultural research policy has several
major components or facets. These include, first, the
amount to invest in research; second, the allocation of
responsibility or opportunity among the potential pro-
viders of research, and, third, the mechanisms for allocating public funds among institutions and among the alternative lines of research. These components are clearly interrelated and the purist might argue that decisions
should be made simultaneously, but there are a number of
reasons why this does not occur.

The amount to be invested in research by the public
sector is generally determined at a different level of
government than the decisions that allocate these funds
among research institutions and/or lines of research.
Consequently the governmental decision process leads to
the result that those who decide if a research institution should exist or those who determine the amount of
money provided to a research institution or project in a
given year act with some degree of independence from each
other as well as from the decisions concerning the total
resources to be provided for agricultural research.

It would simplify matters a great deal if we were
able to say that the amount invested in agricultural re-

search and the allocation of that amount among institutions and research projects would be determined by everywhere equating the expected marginal return to the expected marginal cost of the research. If an optimal amount of investment in research is to be achieved, the expected return should be the social and not the private rate of return. However, there are difficulties with the attribution of the social return. If it is the social return for the citizens of a state or province who have paid the cost of the publicly financed research, the social return for the state or province would be less than for the nation since some of the benefits of the research will be realized by those who live in other states or provinces. But having all agricultural research supported at the national level does not entirely solve the problem; the social return from research as viewed by the world as a whole is significantly higher than the social return for any one country.

I do not put forward lightly the equilibrium condition for the allocation of agricultural research resources. I believe that it is reasonable for national research policies to provide a setting in which it is possible to seek equality of marginal returns and costs in the allocation of resources to agricultural research. Like so many of our prescriptions of the ideal, it is no easy task to achieve the ideal. This does not mean that the ideal is wrong nor that one should not seek the ideal. But it does mean at least two things: One, we should have a considerable degree of empathy for the decision makers who must determine and carry out a national agricultural research policy in a situation where such a high degree of uncertainty prevails; and, two, economists and other researchers have the responsibility of helping to reduce the degree of uncertainty that surrounds the financing of agricultural research.

THE AGRICULTURAL RESEARCH SETTING

In this paper I present ideas concerning the three major components of agricultural research policy and, hopefully, provide a number of suggestions that might assist small developing countries to make more effective use of their research resources. While the major issues to be addressed are how much to invest in research, the institutional settings for conducting the research, and the mechanisms for allocation of research expenditures, there are other topics that should be considered which provide background on the setting within which agricultural research is undertaken. These topics are:

1. differences in agricultural productivity among countries;
2. transferability of agricultural research;

3. sources of borrowing;
4. returns to agricultural research;
5. investment in agricultural research--how much?
6. institutional setting for agricultural research;
7. allocating research funds among institutions and projects;
8. effects of national agricultural policies on agricultural research;
9. an agricultural research policy for a small country.

As the title of this paper indicates, agricultural research policy is considered from the viewpoint of a small developing country. What I have to say applies generally to small countries and not to any particular small country, though some of the material is more directly relevant to countries that are primarily in temperate climatic zones than to countries in the tropics or sub-tropics. This is particularly true of the discussion of transferability of research and the sources of borrowing.

Let me note that I have no precise definition of a small country. In taking special note of the size of a country I have little more in mind than to indicate that the scale of agriculture influences the scale and type of profitable agricultural research. The scale of agriculture also influences the size of research institutions and the size of individual research projects. These are factors that should have a significant influence on agricultural research policy. These considerations become especially significant where there is considerable diversity of climate and thus of economically profitable agricultural enterprises within a country. The United States, France, Indonesia, India and Brazil have the attributes of large countries; the Ivory Coast, Chad, Peru, Haiti and Chile have the attributes of small countries.

Differences in Agricultural Productivity Among Countries

Modern agriculture is of recent origin. The large differences that one now sees in the productivity of land and agricultural labor across countries is also of recent origin. In fact, it is nearly correct to say that modern agriculture is the source of these differences in productivity and that such differences were small prior to the origin of modern agriculture. Modern agriculture is primarily the creature or product of more than a century of organized research and a somewhat longer period of mechanical innovations.

The large differences in land productivity that are now so evident emerged during the last three decades and resulted from the knowledge gained and applied from biological and chemical research, primarily undertaken dur-

ing the twentieth century. Further, the large differences in labor productivity actually emerged earlier, particularly in North America and Western Europe compared to
the rest of the world, as a result of the enormous inven-
tive burst of the late eighteenth and nineteenth centuries in the revolution of mechanical equipment and the
harnessing of power from fossil sources for both station-
ary and moving uses of that power. The differences in
both labor and land productivity in agriculture among
nations in the first half of the nineteenth century were
small. Let us consider some of the evidence on this
point.

Average national or regional grain yields in excess
of two tons per hectare are recent phenomena. In years
of average weather during the first half of this century,
grain yields in the United States averaged less than 1.5
tons per hectare, whereas in recent years average yields
have been 3.5 tons per hectare. Maize yields have increased even more--from 1.4 tons per hectare before 1940
to more than 5.5 tons in recent years (6.4 tons in 1978).

Japan was the only industrial country that achieved
significant increases in grain yields in the nineteenth
century. In the last quarter of the century, Japanese
grain yields increased from 1.3 tons per hectare to 1.9
tons; currently the average yield is a little more than
five tons. Except for Japan, the available evidence indicates that almost all of the yield increases since 1800
have occurred in the last five decades.

For the industrial countries as a group, grain
yields were only 1.15 tons per hectare in 1934-38; in
1975-77, 2.4 tons. In contrast, the average grain yield
for the developing countries was 1.14 tons per hectare in
1934-38, equal to the average for the industrial countries, whereas by 1975-77 the average yield for the developing countries had increased to only 1.6 tons. If
the two giant centrally planned economies, the Soviet
Union and China, are removed from their respective groups,
the average grain yield for the industrial economies during 1927-31 was 1.37 tons per hectare and for the developing countries, 1.15; during 1975-77 the respective yields
were 3.0 and 1.4 tons.

Significant increases in labor productivity, at
least in the United States, occurred a century before the
increases in grain yields. It has been estimated that in
1800 approximately 135 hours of farm labor were used to
produce a ton of corn or wheat; by 1900 the amount of
labor used was 40 hours for wheat and 56 hours for corn.
Forty years later, labor use per ton had declined to 17
and 34 hours for wheat and corn, respectively. Since
1940, the amount of labor used to produce a ton of corn
has decreased by about 90 percent; for wheat by about 80
percent.

Large reductions in labor use per unit of output occurred well before the introduction of the tractor. For
wheat almost 80 percent of the reduction in labor use
during the nineteenth century was due to the reduction in
use of labor during harvest. That century saw the re-
placement of the sickle and cradle by the reaper, the
harvester and the binder, and the introduction of the
combine. For corn most of the reduction of labor use resulted from pre-harvest changes, due mainly to the steel
plow and the horse drawn planter and cultivator.

The differences in labor productivity between the
agricultures of the high and low income countries now
seem so enormous that it is easy to conclude that the
differences can hardly be reduced, let alone eliminated.
Hayami and Ruttan estimated that in 1960 that output per
farm worker in thirteen high income countries was approximately nine times as large as in eleven low income
countries.[5] Yet comparisons presented by them of the
current farm output per worker in low income countries
and the historical path of output per male worker in the
high income countries provide some hope that the huge
differences in labor productivity may be transitory. For
example, agricultural output per worker in the Philippines, Sri Lanka and the United Arab Republic in 1960 was
greater than in Japan in 1881; output per farm worker in
India was approximately the same as in Japan in 1881.
Agricultural output per farm worker in France in 1880 was
approximately matched or exceeded in 1960 in Taiwan, Tur-
key, Peru, Syria, Brazil, Colombia, and Venezuela. Agricultural output per worker in Chile in 1960 equaled that
of France in 1930, Denmark in 1900 and the United States
and the United Kingdom in 1880.[6]

The use of labor per unit of land in the United
States in 1800 can be compared with labor use in India
prior to the adoption of the new high yielding varieties.
In 1800 the use of labor per hectare of wheat in the
United States was 17 days; for the mid-1950s in India the
range was from 32 to 69, with all but one of the seven
examples being less than 42 days. For cotton, labor use
in the United States per hectare in 1800 has been estimated to be 57 days; in India for the mid-1950s the estimates range from 27 to 96 days.[7]

These comparisons hold out the hope that not only
can the current gap in land productivity be closed, but
also that a significant part of the gap in labor productivity can be reduced--not quickly, but over time. In any
case, the data on labor and land productivity indicate
that modern agriculture is a recent, primarily twentieth
century development. Differences that now seem so enormous were much, much smaller in the recent past. Before
the emergence of modern agriculture, agricultural productivity was low throughout the world.[8]

Transferability of Research and Innovation in Agriculture

It was not so long ago that it was believed that a primary source of the differences in productivity between the agricultures of the United States and Western Europe, on the one hand, and the low income countries of Asia and Latin America, on the other hand, was that the farmers of the latter didn't take advantage of the practices of the former. In other words, if others did things the same way we did, they could produce a lot more than they do. This view guided American and other efforts to increase agricultural productivity in Asia by emphasizing extension activities throughout the 1950s and into the 1960s. Extension was to deliver techniques of production that had proved successful under quite different circumstances. I refer not just to economic and social circumstances, but to different climatic and environmental settings.

To some degree the error of assuming that it was relatively easy to transfer technologies from one part of the world to another was understandable. A significant part of the progress of agriculture in Europe and North America was due to borrowing. The potato and many other crops were taken from the Americas to Europe; the wheat varieties that made North America the bread basket of the world were largely borrowed from Russia. Most of the small grain crops grown in North America were brought from Europe. It was not until well into the twentieth century that agricultural research institutions had a major role in modifying and creating crop varieties in Europe and the United States.

Most of the borrowing was from similar climatic areas--from similar latitudes and rainfall and temperature distributions. Many of the attempts during the period of foreign assistance emphasizing extension involved moving varieties and practices from temperate to the semitropical and tropical areas. Very little was the same in the two areas--length of day, distributions of temperatures and rainfall, diseases and insects. In addition, given the differences in economic environment, practices that may have been profitable in North America may not have been profitable in the receiving area.

The examples that I have given indicate that direct borrowing is possible in some circumstances and not in others. More recently we have seen significant borrowing in the new high yielding varieties of wheat and rice. The wheats developed in Mexico have been transferred with considerable success to many parts of the world, including some tropical areas. Its broad adaptability can be attributed, at least in part, to the accidental characteristic of a high degree of photoperiod-insensitivity. This characteristic has meant that these wheats can be

grown at a rather wide variety of latitudes and some of
the spring wheats can be grown as though they were winter
wheats. The new rice varieties also have photoperiod-
insensitivity and are grown over wider latitudinal ranges
than was true of the traditional varieties.

It is not clear whether the new rice and wheat varieties represent more than exceptions to the general rule
that has appeared to emerge in crop research. This rule
is that part of the increased productivity of a number of
economic crops has been due to adapting plants and practices more completely to micro conditions. The emphasis
on adaptation of plants to smaller and smaller geographic
areas reduces the potentialities for transferability.

Obviously there can be substantial cost advantages
in the direct transfer of a crop variety or a production
technique. But there are substantial risks where biology
is involved. Things may go well for a year, two years or
even longer but there is always a high probability that
nature will win in the end. In the U.S. wheat growing
regions, most new varieties have an economic life of approximately five years. In some research done about two
decades ago, Robert Gustafson and I estimated that approximately half of the expenditures on wheat research
was required just to stay even with nature--to repair the
damage done by rusts, viruses and insects.[9] No more than
half of the available effort went to create superior
yielding varieties.

The effective life of most wheat varieties in the
United States is about five years. After a period of
time, yields from a new variety decline due to attacks by
insects or diseases. Evenson has made estimates of the
share of maintenance research in U.S. agricultural research as of the mid-1960s. He estimated that for all
cereals, maintenance research accounted for 40 percent of
the total and for wheat 52 percent. He found that maintenance research accounted for half of all research on
horticultural crops and for 40 percent of the livestock
research.[10] It seems highly likely that much of the
maintenance research should be done in or near the affected farm areas. The need for maintenance research may
go some distance to explain why the profitability of
borrowing increases as research expenditures in the borrowing country increases.

Evenson and Kislev in their Agricultural Research
Productivity deal with the question of the transferability of research.[11] It would be a major benefit to small
countries if it were possible to rely upon others for
most research results and to have a domestic research
enterprise that was largely responsible for drawing from
the available research the most appropriate ideas for the
local conditions. But Evenson and Kislev found that the
benefits of research borrowing is a positive function of

the amount of indigenous research. A country that spends no significant amount on research gains very little from research undertaken in similar climatic zones, while a country that has a significant amount of indigenous research realizes both a direct benefit and a benefit from borrowing. They estimate that the marginal contribution of a research publication in a low income country comes more from accelerated borrowing than from the direct contribution to agricultural productivity.[12] In a later publication, Evenson estimated the benefits to low income countries from research done by others in the same geoclimatic zone. For a low income country with average indigenous research capability, an investment in applied research of $1,000 by others in the same zone resulted in an annual return of $55,000 to the low income country; if the low income country had no indigenous research capability, the return from the same external research investment would be only $1,700 per year to the low income country. Evenson concludes:[13]

> In the developing countries a considerable amount of transfer of benefits based on knowledge diffusion takes place. . . . the calculation shows, however, that such transfer depends heavily on the capacity of indigenous research. The strategy of waiting for the neighbor's technology to "spill in" just doesn't work. The country without an indigenous research capability benefits very little from its neighbor, even when the neighbor is considerate enough to invest in research.

Sources of Borrowing

There are three main sources for borrowing--other developing countries, the industrial countries and the international agricultural research institutes. Small developing countries in the semi-tropical and tropical areas should not neglect the research being undertaken by other developing countries in similar climatic zones. Such research may well be the quickest and easiest to transfer. As the support for agricultural research in the developing countries continues to increase, the opportunities for fruitful borrowing among developing countries will increase. It has been estimated that expenditures on agricultural research in the major developing regions (Latin America, Africa and Asia) increased from $228 million in 1959 to $957 million in 1974 (in 1971 dollars).[14] This represents an annual growth rate of 10 percent or a doubling in just seven years. While scattered evidence indicates a slowing of the growth of agricultural research expenditures in the developing countries, the absolute amount of such research has now reached the point that no developing country can afford to ignore the research results from similarly situated countries.

The international agricultural research institutes have been a major institutional innovation of the past two decades, perhaps the single most important innovation in agricultural institutions in this century. The institutes are mission oriented, generally emphasizing research on one or a small number of agricultural products. The institutes have emphasized the production problems of regions of the world, primarily the tropics and subtropics, that have been relatively neglected in the allocation of the world's agricultural research resources.

The international institutes had an auspicious beginning with the introduction of the new high yielding varieties of wheat by the International Maize and Wheat Improvement Center (CYMMT) of Mexico and of rice by the International Rice Research Institute (IRRI). Actually, the high yielding wheat varieties were created by the joint effort of the Government of Mexico and the Rockefeller Foundation prior to the establishment of CYMMT as an international research institute in 1966.

The successes achieved at IRRI and CYMMT in the development of the new varieties of rice and wheat have not been repeated at the other institutes. The other institutes have been productive as research enterprises, but their results have been less spectacular and have not resulted in varieties or technologies adapted to such large areas of the world.

It needs to be recognized that the international institutes are not adequate substitutes for the development of strong national research institutions in developing countries. One of the hopes for the international institutes was that they would assist in the development of stronger national institutions. While contributions are being made through providing training and maintaining some links with national institutions, much remains to be done by the institutes if they are to succeed in such an effort.

There are now thirteen international agricultural research institutes. The commodities on which research is being undertaken include rice, wheat, corn, barley, triticale, cowpeas, soybeans, lima beans, cassava, yams, sweet potatoes, forages, sorghum, millets, peanuts, pigeon peas, lentils, broad beans, oilseeds, cotton, cattle, swine and sheep. The annual budgets of the institutes now exceed $140 million. The institutes are supported by a consortium of donors, including private foundations, governments and international agencies.

Returns to Agricultural Research

In an article entitled "Economic Benefits from

Table 4.1
Estimates of the return from investment in agricultural research, obtained by using index numbers and regression analysis

Investigator	Year	Country	Commodity	Period	Annual return (%)
Index number					
Griliches	1958	United States	Hybrid corn	1940–1955	35–40
Griliches	1958	United States	Hybrid sorghum	1940–1957	20
Peterson	1967	United States	Poultry	1915–1960	21–25
Evenson	1969	South Africa	Sugarcane	1945–1962	40
Ardito and Barletta	1970	Mexico	Wheat	1943–1963	90
Ardito and Barletta	1970	Mexico	Maize	1943–1963	35
Ayer	1970	Brazil	Cotton	1924–1967	> 77
Schmitz and Schmitz	1970	United States	Tomato harvester	1958–1969	
			With no compensation to displaced workers		37–46
			Assuming compensation of displaced workers for 50 percent of earnings loss		16–28
Scobie and Posada	1978	Colombia	Rice	1957–1964	79–96
Hines	1972	Peru	Maize	1954–1967	35–55
Hayami and Akino	1977	Japan	Rice	1915–1950	25–27
Hayami and Akino	1977	Japan	Rice	1930–1961	73–75
Hertford *et al.*	1977	Colombia	Rice	1957–1972	60–82
		Colombia	Soybeans	1960–1971	79–96
		Colombia	Wheat	1953–1973	11–12
		Colombia	Cotton	1953–1972	None
Peterson and Fitzharris	1977	United States	Aggregate	1937–1942	50
				1947–1952	51
				1957–1962	49
				1957–1972	34
Wennergren and Whitaker	1977	Bolivia	Sheep	1966–1975	44
			Wheat	1966–1975	−48
Regression analysis					
Tang	1963	Japan	Aggregate	1880–1938	35
Griliches	1964	United States	Aggregate	1949–1959	35–40
Latimer	1964	United States	Aggregate	1949–1959	N.S.‡
Peterson	1967	United States	Poultry	1915–1960	21
Evenson	1968	United States	Aggregate	1949–1959	47
Evenson	1969	South Africa	Sugarcane	1945–1958	40
Ardito and Barletta	1970	Mexico	Crops	1943–1963	45–93
Evenson and Jha	1973	India	Aggregate	1953–1971	40
Kahlon *et al.*	1977	India	Aggregate	1960–1961	63
Lu and Cline	1977	United States	Aggregate	1938–1948	30
				1949–1959	28
				1959–1969	26
				1969–1972	24
Bredahl and Peterson	1976	United States	Cash grains	1969	36
			Poultry	1969	37
			Dairy	1969	43
			Livestock	1969	47
Nagy and Furtan	1978	Canada	Rapeseed	1960–1975	95–110
Evenson and Flores	1978	Asia-national	Rice	1950–1965	32–39
Flores, Evenson, and Hayami	1976	Philippines	Rice	1966–1975	27
Flores, Evenson, and Hayami	1976	Tropics	Rice	1966–1975	46–71
Evenson and Flores	1978	Asia-national	Rice	1966–1975	73–78
Evenson and Flores	1978	Asia-international	Rice	1966–1975	74–102

Source: Robert E. Evenson, Paul E. Waggoner and Vernon W. Ruttan, "Economic Benefits from Research: An Example from Agriculture," SCIENCE, Vol. 205, 14 September 1980, p. 1103.

Research: An Example from Agriculture," Evenson, Waggoner and Ruttan summarize much of the available evidence on the returns to agricultural research.[15] Estimated rates of return are available from studies for the United States, Japan, India, the Philippines, five countries in Latin America and internationally sponsored research centers are presented in Table 1. The studies in the table are arranged in two categories--one classified as "index numbers" and the other as "regression analysis." Their explanation of the two categories follows:[16]

The estimates classified as "index number" were computed directly from the cost of research on, say, hybrid corn, and the benefits were obtained from the estimated increase in production attributed by hybrid corn. Typically, the benefits and costs were assumed to continue indefinitely. The calculated returns of 20 to 90 percent are the average returns for every dollar invested. In these studies benefits are defined as the benefits for both producers and consumers.
The estimates classified as "regression analysis" were computed by a different method that permits estimation of the return from increased investment rather than the average return from all investment. Further, this method can assign parts of the return to different sources, such as scientific research and extension advice. Because regression methods are used, the significance of the estimated returns from research can be tested statistically. The dependent variable as the change in total productivity, and benefit is defined as the value of the change in productivity. The independent variables include research variables, which reflect the cost of research and the lag between investment and benefit. The objective of the regression procedure is to estimate that component of the change in productivity that can be attributed to research.

As will be noted from analysis of the table almost all of the estimated rates of return are greater than 20 percent and several are 50 percent or larger. While there have been expressions of disbelief concerning the magnitudes of the rates of return, I have seen no systematic critique of the results that makes a plausible case for disregarding the conclusion that the rates of return from agricultural research have been large compared to rates of return on most public or private investments.[17]
There are two questions that the skeptic can ask about the rate of return estimates. One is why the rates appear to be approximately the same across countries faced by substantial differences in current and past rates of investment in research. The other is why the countries do not invest significantly more than they do in agricul-

tural research if rates of return are so high. Let us consider these two questions or reservations.

One gains a clear impression from inspection of Table 2 that the rates of return from research appear to be approximately the same for a wide range of accumulated or annual expenditures on research or for wide differences in agricultural technology. This similarity may raise a question about the validity of the estimates. However, John Antle in his important contribution "Human Capital, Infrastructure and Technology Choice in Agricultural Development" provides significant explanation of the apparent constancy of average or marginal returns from research.

Antle analyzed the effects of human capital and infrastructural capital upon agricultural productivity. His study was based upon a cross-country analysis of productivity, similar to that of Hayami and Ruttan, but with additional variables to measure the infrastructure relevant to agriculture for each country. These variables included transport costs, education, and research expenditures or proxies for these variables. He applied a similar approach to individual farm data for Indian rice producers, adding credit costs, extension services and high yielding varieties as variables. He found that the choice of technology by farms and level of productivity were significantly affected by their economic environment, including the infrastructure of the country or community. He concludes[17]

> that the benefits obtainable from investments in education, extension programs, and agricultural research may be seriously limited if the complementary infrastructure investments are not made.

This result seems so obvious that one can only express surprise that the interrelationships have received so little previous analysis and study.

The second question raises doubt about the high rates of return; if the rates are so high, isn't it unreasonable that the investment in research should be so small? As pointed out earlier, an important reason that marginal social returns exceed marginal cost is that only part of the research benefits are realized by the agency making the expenditures. For example, in the United States, the majority of the public funds expended on agricultural research comes from the states; federal expenditures supplement state funds. As a result, it is reasonable to assume that the allocation of state funds to agricultural research will be based upon the returns realized by that state from the research undertaken. Evenson has estimated the returns to state supported agricultural research for three different periods between 1868 and 1971. As a part of that analysis, he estimated the percentage of the benefits realized by the state undertaking the research, as measured by productivity change in agriculture attributed to the research done in each state for each time period. His results, including estimates of the rates of return to research, are given in Table 2.

The percentage of the benefits realized by the state undertaking the research ranges from only 32 percent for science-oriented research to 100 percent for farm management and agricultural extension. On the average, it would appear that about half of the benefits go to states other than those undertaking the research. If this estimate is accepted, then a 50 percent social rate of return to research becomes only a 25 percent return to the state paying for the research.

But even this loss of half of the benefits from research is not all of the story. Evenson's dependent variable--the measure of the benefit from research--is the change in factor productivity attributed to the research. It is now generally recognized that a large percentage of the benefit from agricultural productivity growth redounds to the benefit of consumers. Thus a state that is a major producer of agricultural products but one with a relatively small population will find that most of the benefits from research go to consumers elsewhere in the country and in the world.

While federal or national support of agricultural research will help overcome some of the underinvestment in research, such an approach to the financing of research does not fully solve the problem. Even for a country as large as the United States or India, a significant part of the benefits from agricultural research go to "the rest of the world." Evenson has estimated that for the developed countries well over half of the benefits from agricultural research is contributed to other countries; a somewhat larger transfer of benefits was estimated for developing countries.[18] And since these estimates did not take into account the price effects of increased agricultural output resulting from agricultural research, the estimates do not reflect the transfers of benefits to consumers both within the country and outside it.

The fact that a large share of the benefits of agricultural research is realized by others than those who pay for that research is, to some degree, the reverse side of the question transferability of research. If research can be transferred, some of its benefits will be realized by others than those who undertook the research. The earlier discussion of the extent of transfer of research and technology emphasized the benefits from borrowing are a positive function of the amount of research done in the borrowing country. The emphasis in this part of the paper is to look at the question of distribution of benefits of agricultural research in terms of its effects upon the amount invested in such research.

Table 4.2 Estimated returns from agricultural research in the United States, 1868 to 1971, with percentage
of benefits realized in State undertaking the research.

Subject	Maximum Annual Benefit from $1000 Invest- ment (dollars)	Annual Rate of Return (%)	Percentage of Benefits Realized in State Undertaking the Research
	1868 to 1926		
All agricultural research	12,500	65	Not estimated
	1927 to 1950		
Agricultural research			
Technology-oriented	11,400	95	55
Science-oriented	53,000	110	33
	1948 to 1971		
Agricultural research			
Technology-oriented			
South	21,000	130	67
North	11,600	93	43
West	12,200	95	67
Science-oriented	4,500	45	32
Farm management and agri- cultural extension	2,173	110	100

Source: Robert E. Evenson, Paul E. Waggoner and Vernon W. Ruttan, "Economic Benefits from Research: An Example from Agriculture," SCIENCE, Vol. 205, 14 September 1979, p. 1105.

There is no conflict between the two points of view and
both have important implications for decisions that affect
the amount of agricultural research actually undertaken.

Investment in Agricultural Research--How Much?

In any country there is a group of responsible individuals who must decide how much public money should be
invested in agricultural research. In the United States
there are many such groups of responsible individuals--at
least one group in each state plus various branches of
the federal government. In countries with highly central-
ized governments there may be one key group in the national capital. But whether there are one or many groups,
the problems remain pretty much the same. As I hope is
now clear, the decision on the annual expenditure of public funds on agriculture research is both complex and
difficult. While ideally a government would want to ex-
pend that amount at which the marginal benefit equals the
marginal cost, it is far from easy to arrive at that
point. Whose marginal benefit? Should any weight be
given to the benefits derived by other countries? Should
benefits that go to consumers within the country be given
the same weight as benefits or losses accruing to land
owners, farm workers, and input supply industries?

Whenever a government expends additional funds on agricultural research, it will have an effect upon private
expenditures on research relevant to agriculture. Generally it might be expected that additional public expenditures would be partially offset by smaller private expenditures, though this effect may be offset in whole or in
part if the results of publicly supported agricultural
research open up substantial new opportunities for research and development in the private sector. This
clearly seems to have been the case with hybrid corn in
the United States. Large private research expenditures
on hybrid corn did not happen by accident, but was the
result of policy decisions that left the corn seed industry with a minimum of governmental regulation plus decisions by the public research sector to undertake research that was complementary to that of the private sector rather than was a substitute for it. But whether
public expenditures are substitutes or complements for
private expenditures, decisions on public research expenditures should take this relationship into account.

I have no magic technique that makes it easy for a decision maker to decide how much public money should be
spent on agricultural research. I believe that <u>the evidence presented on the returns to agricultural research
definitely supports the position that a given country
should spend no less as a percentage of the value of its
agricultural output than is now being spent by the average of countries with comparable levels of income</u>. In

82

1974 countries with per capita incomes in excess of
$1,000 had research and extension expenditures of about
2.4 percent of the value of agricultural output.[19] With
reasonable effectiveness in execution, this minimum level
of expenditure on agricultural research and extension
would assure a rate of return on research substantially
above the rate generally produced by governmental expenditures.

How much more than this amount could be justified
depends upon a number of factors that I can only note,
though I will return to some of them in the concluding
section of the paper. The factors not noted above that
would affect the desired level of public expenditure on
agricultural research include the diversity of climatic
and soil conditions, the number of different crops and
animals that are economically important, the possibility
of borrowing research results and technology, and the appropriate division of the effort between basic and applied research.

Institutional Settings for Agricultural Research

At a workshop held at the University of Chicago in
late 1977, Vernon Ruttan commented upon a paper by Robert
Evenson, "The Organization of Research to Improve Crops
and Animals in Low-income Countries." In his comments,
Ruttan emphasized three major unsettled questions concerning the conduct of agricultural research.[21]
The first of the questions was that of the location
of agricultural research stations. Here there are two
not very closely related aspects--the geographic location
of a research station and its location relative to other
institutions. For a particular country, the issue of
geographic location is related to the nature of the research on the spectrum from basic to applied and the problems that require solution. Such location decisions
must also be influenced by whether there are significant
scale economies in agricultural research. There has been
little systematic analysis of productivity of research
stations as a function of their relationship to other institutions. Most of us in the United States believe that
the most productive agricultural research stations are
those associated with colleges and universities. However,
throughout much of Europe and South America agricultural
research institutions are separate research institutes
with little or no tie to an educational institution.
Ruttan's second unsettled issue was that of the relationship between scale and productivity in agricultural
research. There is some evidence that is mildly optimis-
tic for small countries, namely that under some circumstances, output per scientific worker has been very high
in agricultural research institutions with fewer than
twenty scientific or technical staff.[22] In any case,

significant increasing returns to scale for agricultural research does not seem to be supported by the evidence, though much more analysis is required before one can support the opposite view.

The third unsettled issue raised by Ruttan is concerned with the organization and structure of agricultural research. In his brief discussion Ruttan emphasizes primarily the internal organization of research activities along disciplinary or multidisciplinary lines. In the United States, both the national research system and the university-based state systems have evolved into disciplinary structures while both systems generally started out as multidisciplinary units in their early years when much of the research was more technologically oriented than is the case today. But there are other unsettled issues concerning the organization and structure of agricultural research. One noted earlier is the alternative of separate institutes versus integration into a university alongside teaching and extension. Another issue is whether the research institutions should be national or regional (state) in terms of their control and financing or whether some mixed system should emerge.

The previous paragraphs have emphasized a couple of fairly simple points. One is that there is insufficient evidence to permit one to be dogmatically assured about numerous aspects of the organization and location of agricultural research within a country. The other point is that there is sufficient evidence to indicate that there are high rates of return to agricultural research under numerous institutional arrangements--public and private, national and regional, research institute and university-based--that the desirability of getting on with the support of agricultural research should not be delayed too much by time spent trying to devise the perfect system. I do not want to be interpreted as saying that there is any system of agricultural research that exists that could not be improved and institutional change may be one of the avenues for improvement. What I am saying is that some degree of dissatisfaction with a particular set of institutional and financing arrangements should not be permitted to interfere with the most effective use of the existing arrangements. This is particularly true in light of the decline in the real level of support for agricultural research around the world during the 1970s.

There are three additional points that may appear to be obvious, yet failure to deal with any one of these three points may result in significant limitations on the effectiveness of the funds actually allocated. The first point is that the logistical support for agricultural research should be given a high priority. In many developing countries, needed supplies and equipment cannot be obtained at all or are very slow in delivery. The availability of equipment and supplies may be limited by exchange controls or simply the slowness of the bureaucratic process surrounding governmental procurement. Whatever the reasons, the effectiveness of funds spent on agricultural research is reduced by such failures.

The second point is concerned with the framework of accountability imposed upon agricultural research institutions. In many countries, a large paperwork burden is imposed upon research institutions in accounting for all funds, equipment and construction, but the more important tasks of specifying broad research priorities and monitoring ongoing research activities are often neglected. Close contacts between the appropriate authorities in agriculture and finance ministries and research institutions can be much more effective in establishing accountability than a host of regulations.

Finally, strong agricultural research institutions depend upon levels of remuneration for scientists and other personnel adequate to attract and retain highly competent individuals. In all too many countries the financial rewards for individuals with research skills are much greater in the governmental bureaucracies or in the private sectors than in agricultural research and educational institutions. Consequently, even those who are highly motivated to use their research skills often find it much more advantageous to move into other activities in either the private or public sector. All too often, agricultural research institutions are located in communities that have relatively few amenities to attract and hold the well educated. Thus it is not too surprising that a combination of relatively low pay and limited social and cultural opportunities cause many competent agricultural scientists to move to the larger cities.

Allocating Research Funds

An unsettled question not directly delineated by Ruttan is that of the most appropriate way of allocating available public funds among institutions and projects. These allocations are made in a multitude of ways around the world and, even within the United States, numerous formulae and procedures are used in the public sector. Some federal funds given to the states are allocated by a formula; other allocations among types of research have been determined very largely by legislative enactment; still other funds are allocated as the result of competition for grants or contracts with awards being made primarily on the basis of peer review.

The methods of providing public support for agricultural research in the United States cannot be said to be very systematic and there is undoubtedly duplication of effort in the process. Yet I hold rather firmly to the opinion that monopoly in agricultural research support or in the conduct of such research is as bad as monopoly in any sector of the economy. As a result, I am firmly of the opinion that efforts should be made to introduce a significant element of competition in both the allocation of funds and in the conduct of agricultural research.

A large country can afford to introduce competition in the sources of public funds for supporting agricultural research. However, this becomes much more problematic for a small country that may have limited administrative resources that may be best used to staff a single national research agency or a single agency for each of the major sectors of the economy. Nonetheless, it may be desirable in a small country to introduce competition in the procedures for allocating funds among institutions and/or projects. There is more than adequate evidence to support the view that a nation runs great risks when it permits the idiosyncratic views of an individual or a small number of individuals to dominate the conduct of science or the choice of scientific methods and significant problems.

There is no simple answer to how competition can be introduced. Peer review of project proposals is an approach that has been adopted by most of the major governmental research supporting agencies in the United States. The system is not without its critics, though much of the criticism comes from those who believe peer review results in an elitist outcome in the allocation of research funds. If peer review works well and the recommendations made are followed by the bureaucrats, it is inevitable that it should have elitist consequences.

While the peer review process can be used for both the evaluation of the research programs of an institution and particular projects, most research funds allocated through a peer review process in the United States are for particular projects. There are those who would argue that the project approach results in waste and resource misallocation, primarily since our national urge for accountability is requiring increasingly detailed and frequent proposals.

But no system of allocating funds can or should remove all of responsibilities from the political process. The priorities for the major aspects of research will be determined by the same process that allocates funds among various types of social welfare programs or different levels of education. Not only will political decisions determine the total amount of funds available for agricultural research, but the allocation of funds among broad categories of research (crops and animals, for example) may be either implicitly or explicitly determined through the appropriation process. There is no doubt that the allocation of research funds is influenced by the political process and it is inevitable that this should be the case. But the specific system of allocation of research funds should minimize the role of the political process where it has no competence, namely in matters of scientific theory, method, and appropriate research procedures.

It is desirable that the process of allocating research funds recognize the needs and requirements of those who have relatively little political influence. In many developing countries certain crops are grown primarily by small and low income farmers, often located in places quite distant from the major city. In too many cases food crops important to this large segment of the population have been neglected in the allocation of research effort.

National Policies and the Benefits from Agricultural Research

In the final analysis, the benefits that any country, be it a small or a large country, can obtain from the world's stock of relevant scientific and technological knowledge will depend both upon the policies directly related to the conduct of agricultural research and those policies that influence the use of agricultural resources in the economy. It is important to note the significance of general national agricultural policy.

The agricultural research that is undertaken is influenced by the setting in which that research is conducted. Researchers and research institutions respond to the circumstances and the environment within which they operate. Consequently national agricultural policies, such as price supports, input subsidies, or taxes, influence the nature of research and the potential social benefits from that research. National policies that result in distortions in the allocation of agricultural resources compound such distortions by influencing research efforts.

Ruttan and Hayami have given strong support to the view that agricultural research and innovation are induced:[23] the research undertaken and innovations introduced respond to profitability. Research institutions consider the relative scarcity of resources and the potential for saving the scarcest resources that might be accomplished through research. Similarly, in their decision concerning what innovations or new methods of production to adopt, farmers clearly take into account the effect of an innovation or new production method upon their profits or income. Consequently, if national agricultural policies distort price relationships over a period of time, research efforts will be misdirected. The misdirection or inefficient allocation can be that either too much or too little is invested in a particular line of research. Examples of each outcome can be given.

An overvalued currency acts as a tax on exports. In developing countries the primary source of export earn-

ings consists of one or more agricultural products. An
overvalued currency reduces the profitability of such export products and, in consequence, reduces the incentive
to devote research resources to improve productivity of
the inputs used to produce agricultural export products.
Numerous developing countries also impose export taxes.
A report of the Comptroller General of the United States
listed 19 developing countries that imposed export taxes
upon one or more agricultural products in the mid-1970s.[24]

Thailand was one of the countries with an export tax
on a major food grain, rice. A study of rice price
policy in Thailand by Chung Ming Wong indicated that the
export tax reduced the production of rice during the
1960s by as much as 1.5 million tons or nearly 15 percent.[25] The export tax resulted in large income transfers from farmers to consumers and taxpayers, amounting
to 5 to 8 percent of national income. After noting the
static welfare effects of the rice export tax, Wong continues:[26] "... the dynamic effects of the premium on the
rice-producing sector should not be forgotten. The rice
premium represents a substantial burden on the poor farmers. Objections on equity grounds aside, it is quite
possible that the export (tax), by keeping the price of
rice low, may lower the farmer's incentive to improve
yield by adopting modern inputs (fertilizers, high-
yielding varieties of rice) in paddy production, thus
shifting to a higher production function. It is perhaps
because of this that the paddy yield in Thailand is low
when compared with most other countries..." Only 11 percent of the Thailand rice area was seeded to the high
yielding rice varieties compared to more than a third in
India and Pakistan.[27] The only Asian country for which
data are available that had a lower percentage of its
total rice area devoted to high yielding varieties than
Thailand in 1976/77 was Burma. Obviously factors other
than the rice export tax were responsible for the low
rate of adoption of the high yielding varieties in Thailand. However, the relatively low rice price had a negative effect both upon farmers in making investments required to adopt the new varieties and upon researchers
who recongize that the distorted rice price makes the
private benefits from rice research very low, indeed.
Until farmers can afford to make the investments and pay
the higher current costs associated with the new varieties, the potential social benefits cannot be realized.

Another output discouraging measure is the control
of domestic prices for the benefit of consumers. Export
taxes reduce domestic prices and the use of price ceil-
ings and subsidized imports can have the same consequence.
For the past 15 years, India has followed a policy of
holding the domestic price of rice below the world price.
Vasant A. Sukhatme found that for 1967 through 1972 (the
period of rapid adoption of the new rice varieties) the

domestic wholesale price of milled rice averaged 25 percent below the unit value or price of imported rice.
This relationship existed even when the official rate of
exchange is used in the comparison.[28] Since the rupee
was significantly overvalued during this period, the real
domestic price of rice might have been as much as 50 percent below the world price. During the same period of
time, the internal price of wheat in India, after cor-
recting for the overvaluation of the rupee, was very
close to the world price--perhaps 8 percent above. In
1976/77 it was estimated that almost 72 percent of all
wheat planted in India was high yield varieties while
only 36 percent of the rice was in high yielding varieties.[29] Sukhatme's research indicates that a large part
of the difference was the result of the differential
price treatment.[30] It is not obvious that the Indian
consumer will gain in the long run from a policy of
"cheap" rice.

The responsiveness of research institutions to national farm price policies can be seen from the allocation of agricultural research resources in Japan. Japan
has maintained the farm price of rice substantially a-
bove the world price, currently more than three times the
world price. The high price has resulted in the production of more rice than is consumed domestically, even
though the consumer price of rice is but a minor fraction
of the price paid to the farmers. Japan has introduced
acreage limitation programs and large subsidies to induce
farmers to produce crops other than rice. But the experiment stations, especially those supported by prefecture
or local governments, have continued to increase their
expenditures on rice research even though the social
value of that research is negative. Quite properly, the
local experiment stations respond primarily to the potential for private benefits to the farmers in their locality. Given the national rice policy, private benefits
of rice production and rice research remain very large.

Keijiro Otsuka concluded his study of the effects of
the rice pricing policy upon the allocation of agricultural research resources as follows:[31] "In this study we
have identified a strong impact of the supported rice
price on research resource allocations in the public sector. Market prices, even though distorted by government,
transmit the profit information to producers. They will,
in response to the market prices, press the government to
allocate public resources." He goes on to state that the
amount of research undertaken on rice was not socially
optimal, but that too many resources were devoted to rice
research. In the long run the misallocation of research
efforts could have a negative impact on the growth of agricultural productivity:[32] "Furthermore, considering
that public sectors are deep-seated in the provision of
research, extension, and irrigation, a distorted market

price could have very great impacts on the future of agricultural productivity growth. In developing countries, where the product prices are depressed and prices of modern inputs are politically supported, agricultural growth may well have been slowed by bad investments of public resources."

Very little needs to be added to Mr. Otsuka's conclusions. His work supports the conclusion that public research institutions respond to the market incentives provided to farmers. When governments manipulate farm prices, they do more--much more--than influence decisions made by farmers in the allocation of their resources. The manipulation of farm prices affects many public decisions, such as how much to invest in agricultural research and how the agricultural research is allocated among various farm products. And where there is an important private sector that provides inputs to agriculture, decisions in that sector are significantly influenced by the prices of farm products.

Thus all countries, developing and industrial, low income and high income, should consider the interrelationships between national agricultural price and income policies and their agricultural research policies. The evidence is very clear that there exists a strong impact of the price and income policies upon the social effectiveness of agricultural research. All too often the price and income policies result in a significant loss of the potential benefits of agricultural research.

Research Policy for a Small Country

I shall conclude by suggesting some considerations that are relevant to the policy for agricultural research for a small country. A small country is favored if its climate is similar to that of certain major agricultural areas in temperate climatic areas. This means that there exists a large knowledge and technology base that is available for transfer, with appropriate adaptation, to the conditions prevailing in the small country. Small countries in the tropics do not have this advantage since the pool of relevant research and technology for the tropics is far more limited than for the temperate zones.

The implication of climatic comparisons for agricultural research policy is that for a period of some years research policy should be designed to maximize the benefits from adaptive research--research that will build on work done elsewhere. It is not intended that all agricultural research be of an applied and adaptive character. Some emphasis upon more science-oriented research is desirable in order to provide training and to maintain the interest of highly qualified individuals. Many, if not most, of the problems that must be solved by adaptive research require competence in the basic biological

sciences for their solution. The capacity in these
sciences should not be lost by total concentration upon
quick results from adaptive research.

Another aspect of agricultural research policy is
the appropriate role of the private for-profit sector.
As noted earlier, except in North America, very little
agricultural research is undertaken by the industrial or
for-profit sector. Again, except for North America, very
little agricultural research is undertaken by the private
not-for-profit sector, primarily because such a sector is
of little significance in most countries. Substantial
research and development effort is undertaken by industrial firms in North America; there is very little that
can be classified as research carried out by individual
farms except, perhaps, on farms that are owned by large
agribusiness firms. Research undertaken in the private
sector in North America is primarily for the development
or improvement of products--seeds, insecticides, herbicides, fertilizer, machinery--that firms anticipate sell-
ing in sufficient quantity and at a price to provide a
positive return on the research investment. One reason,
though I think not the only one, for the concentration
in North America of much of the world's research by for
profit firms is the large size of the North American market. Support of research by industrial firms in small
countries is likely to be at a very modest level. This
leads to the conclusion that, in a small country, even
most highly applied agricultural research will have to be
financed from public funds. Failure to do so will mean
that such research will not be undertaken and substantial
opportunities for social gain will have been foregone.

A major element in the research policy of a small
country should be providing for effective competition a-
mong viable research organizations. I assume that most
of the costs of agricultural research must come from public funds. But if those funds are to be used effectively,
there should be competition for them. Research organizations can be of several types: University based, government operated, private not for profit, and private for
profit. As I have argued above, I doubt if the private
for profit research enterprises can be of much significance in a small country unless such research is subsidized through governmental funds. If more than one type
of research organization exists, governmental funding
should be even-handed, providing for payment of the same
share of research costs and for equal access to the available funds based on anticipated productivity. In other
words, the criteria used for determining governmental
payments for the support of research should not favor one
type of reseasrch organization over another.

I have earlier referred with favor to the desirable
role of peer review as a technique for deciding upon the
allocation of public funds among organizations and re-

search projects. Some might argue that in a small
country the peer review system is of limited value due to
the relatively small number of competent peers in any
given area of research. If this is an issue, at least
one remedy is available: research proposals could be
sent to reviewers in other countries, or one or more members of a review panel could be drawn from the international research community. Obtaining external opinions
on research proposals would not be difficult nor expensive. A great deal can be accomplished by mail.

My concluding comment will be about the level of research expenditures in a small country. Earlier I noted
that one point of reference was the percentage of the
value of agricultural output expended upon agricultural
research or agricultural research and extension by
countries of comparable per capita incomes. Given the
strong evidence that the marginal return on agricultural
research investment is generally higher than the marginal
return on other public or private investments, the percentage of the value of agricultural output could be
reasonably considered a minimum.

I wish to suggest that a small country, if most of
its agricultural research is applied research, has an opportunity to break new ground in the planning and financing of agricultural research, namely to establish a practice of making ex ante estimates of the social returns
and costs of research. While such ex ante estimates
should have some role in the allocation of research resources, the primary role would be to serve as guides for
the determination of the total amount to be spent on agricultural research. Obviously, the ex ante estimates
will merit a significant role in decision making only if,
on the average, ex post estimates equal or exceed the ex
ante estimates.

Footnotes

1. Yujiro Hayami and Ruttan, Vernon W., Agricultural Development: An International Perspective (Baltimore: The Johns Hopkins Press, 1971), pp. 137-38.
2. Ibid., p. 137.
3. Harry G. Johnson, Technology and Economic Interdependence (London: Macmillan, 1975), p. 13.
4. Robert E. Evenson, "The Contribution of Agricultural Research and Extension to Agricultural Production" (Ph.D. dissertation, The University of Chicago, 1968), p. 3. In a later article "Comparative Evidence on Returns to Investment in National and International Research Institutions" in Resource Allocation and Productivity in National and International Agricultural Research, edited by Thomas M. Arndt, Dana G. Dalrymple, and Vernon W. Ruttan (Minneapolis: University of Minnesota Press, 1977), he estimates that 25.4 percent of agricultural research expenditures in North America in 1974 was accounted for by the industrial sector (p. 255).
5. Hayami and Ruttan, op. cit., p. 97.
6. Ibid., pp. 78-80.
7. Sources: Martin R. Cooper, Glen T. Barton and Albert P. Brodell, Progress of Farm Mechanization, U.S. Department of Agriculture, Misc. Pub. No. 630, 1947, p.3. U. S. Department of Agriculture, Agricultural Statistics 1977, p. 449, and Shakuntla Mehra, Some Aspects of Labour Use in Indian Agriculture, Department of Agricultural Economics, Cornell University, Occasional Paper No. 88, June 1976. The higher estimate of labor days for cotton in India includes both irrigated and unirrigated land; the lower estimate only unirrigated. All U.S. farm land in 1800 would have been unirrigated. In the mid-1970s the use of farm labor per hectare of cotton land in the United States was about seven days. By 1900 labor use in producing cotton per unit of output had declined by about 50 percent compared to a century earlier.
8. The history of famines in Europe provides another indication of the recent origins of the current levels of land and labor productivity. Famines occurred in Western Europe well into the eighteenth century; the 1769 famine in France was one of the worst in history in terms of its estimated loss of life. Ireland had its great famines as late as 1850. The Soviet Union suffered two famines after World War I. The twentieth century has witnessed a remarkable decline in the incidence of famines, though the reasons for the decline are to be found more in improved communication and transportation than in increased food production per capita in the low income

countries.

9. D. Gale Johnson and Robert L. Gustafson, <u>Grain Yields and the American Food Supply: An Analysis of Yield Changes and Possibilities</u> (Chicago: The University of Chicago Press, 1962), p. 120.

10. Robert E. Evenson, "Research, Invention, Extension and Productivity Change in U.S. Agriculture: An Historical Decomposition Analysis." Paper prepared for Symposium on Agricultural Research and Extension Evaluation, Moscow, Idaho, May 21-23, 1978, p. 40.

11. Robert E. Evenson and Yoav Kislev, <u>Agricultural Research and Productivity</u> (New Haven: Yale University Press, 1975), Chap. 4.

12. <u>Ibid.</u>, p. 75.

13. Robert E. Evenson in Arndt, Dalrymple and Ruttan, <u>op. cit.</u>, p. 250.

14. <u>Ibid.</u>, p. 255.

15. Robert E. Evenson, Paul E. Waggoner and Vernon W. Ruttan, "Economic Benefits from Research: An Example from Agriculture," SCIENCE, Vol. 205, 14 September 1979, pp. 1103.

16. <u>Ibid.</u>, p. 1102.

17. <u>The Review of Marketing and Agricultural Economics</u> contains a number of articles dealing with the magnitude of research benefits and how these benefits are distributed between producers and consumers. These articles (by Grant M. Scobie, Vol. 44, No. 4, December 1976; F. G. Jarrett and R. K. Lindner, Vol. 45, No. 4, December 1977) note that there were ambiguities in the formula for measured benefits in some of the earlier studies, but there seemed to be no systematic effect of these ambiguities upon the magnitude of the benefits. The most serious criticism made is that the measurement of benefits depends upon assumptions about the shapes and positions of the supply functions from the origin to the equilibrium points for supply and demand for both the before and after situations. Where the supply functions used are estimated econometrically, the elasticity estimates are not valid for points far from the range covered by the actual data. In fact, most of the estimates of research benefits in Appendix A derived from the index number approach were assumed by the researchers. The criticisms made in the articles referred to do not apply to research benefits estimated by the regression approach.

18. John Antle, "Human Capital, Infrastructure, and Technology Choice in Agricultural Development" (Ph.D. dissertation, The University of Chicago, 1980), p. 50.

19. Arndt, Dalrymple and Ruttan, <u>op. cit.</u>, p. 250.

20. <u>Ibid.</u>, p. 256.

21. In Theodore W. Schultz, ed., <u>Distortions of Agricultural Incentives</u> (Bloomington: Indiana University Press, 1978), pp. 246-53.

22. <u>Ibid.</u>, p. 250.

23. Hayami and Ruttan, op. cit., especially Chapters 3 and 8.

24. Comptroller General of the United States, Disincentives to Agricultural Production in Developing Countries, Report to the Congress, ID-76-2, November 26, 1975.

25. Chung Ming Wong, "A Model of the Rice Economy of Thailand" (Ph.D. dissertation, The University of Chicago, 1976), p. 53.

26. Chung Ming Wong, "A Model for Evaluating the Effects of the Thai Government Taxation of Rice Exports on Trade and Walfare," American Journal of Agricultural Economics 60, No. 1 (February 1978), p. 73.

27. Dana G. Dalrymple, Development and Spread of High-Yielding Varieties of Wheat and Rice in the Less Developed Nations, U.S. Department of Agriculture, Foreign Agricultural Economic Report No. 95, 6th ed., September 1978, p. 125.

28. Vasant A. Sukhatme, "The Utilization of High-Yielding Rice and Wheat Varieties in India: An Economic Assessment" (Ph.D. dissertation, The University of Chicago, 1976).

29. Ibid.

30. Ibid.

31. Keijiro Otsuka, "Allocation of Public Resources to Agricultural Research: Japan 1950-75 with Reference to the Pricing of Rice" (Ph.D. dissertation, The University of Chicago, 1979), p. 47.

32. Ibid., p. 48.

5
Socially Efficient Development and Allocation of Water in Developing Countries: Roles for the Public and Private Sectors

Charles W. Howe

INTRODUCTION

Water systems have features that are unique among all the renewable resource systems, especially the inter-dependence among users of the resource. While these special features pose particular challenges for the socially efficient administration of the resource, it must not be inferred that water is different from other economic resources nor that the usual principles of efficient allocation cannot be applied to water. They can—with appropriate modification.

The widespread public belief that water is different and subject to a unique set of rules has had a mischie-vous effect on water administration, for it has facilita-ted the approval of grossly inefficient projects and the serving of narrow, special interests by publicly fin-anced projects. People have been far too ready to leap from the "necessity of water to life" (4 liters per day) to the necessity of building massive projects for irriga-tion, navigation, or power.

It is true, however, that the unique features of water systems create particularly difficult problems that can be solved in nearly all settings only by the inter-vention of government at some level: local, regional, or national. At the same time, the private sector has unique advantages in making certain micro-level decisions --advantages based on detailed information about individ-ual economic opportunities.

Thus, there is a range for the distribution of re-sponsibilities for water development and management be-tween public and private sectors. This Chapter attempts to delimit that range by describing the unique features of water systems and their implications for socially ef-ficient decision-making regarding water resources.

UNIQUE FEATURES OF WATER RESOURCE SYSTEMS

The river basin as the natural management unit

A river basin consists of a complex of directly con-
nected drainage basins tributary to a main river. Under
natural conditions, all of the water in the river origin-
ates in the basin. Certain subsets of users, namely
those that stand in a "downstream relationship" to others
are dependent on the actions of those upstream. As we
will note below, these interdependencies greatly complicate managing the water of the basin. However, the river
basin remains the natural unit within which to solve
these problems.

How far does one river basin extend for purposes of
optimum management? The world's ten longest rivers range
from 6650 km. (the Nile) to 4400 km. (the Lena, USSR).
In many cases, major rivers are tributary to others, as
the Missouri (3726 km., USA) is tributary to the Mississ-
ippi (3779 km., USA). The river basin is a natural management unit because it encompasses most of the externalities that will occur from water uses, but the administrative awkwardness of larger areas comes to offset the
advantages of more completely encompassing all the externalities. The resultant choice of area for management
purposes is a compromise. Figure 1 illustrates the major
river basins of the United States and their relationship
to the state boundaries.

Figure 5.1

The States and Major River Basins
of the United States

From the administrative and legal viewpoints, there
are advantages in defining the river basin administrative
unit along the boundaries of political units, recognition
being given to economic connectedness, too. In Figure 1
it can be seen that the Missouri Basin covers parts of 10
states. These states have different types of water law
and, to some extent, conflicting interests over the basin's resources. Statistical data as well as the authority to tax generally exist at the state level. Thus, it
would in many cases be optimal to define the river basin
along state lines rather than strictly on hydrologic
grounds.

Economic relations across river basin divides may be
strong enough that the extra-basin economic area should
be included in the basin for planning purposes. Southern
California gets 50 percent of its water from the Lower
Colorado and the Denver Metropolitan Area gets at least
that much of its water from the Upper Colorado. While
management policies for the Colorado River directly affect these important areas, they are not part of the Colorado River Basin. Again, the optimum area for planning
and administration will be a compromise among these factors.

Interdependence of users

In popular literature, water is frequently referred
to as a "fugitive resource," not meaning that it can't be
captured but that it flows and meanders and thereby
creates connections among those parties who would use it.
Flow interdependencies are obvious: if upstream parties
consume large quantities or badly pollute the river,
those below will have less and suffer damages from pollution. If reservoirs release water in large surges, downstream parties may experience flooding, navigational difficulties, and the destruction of fisheries.

There also exist what we might call volume or stock
interdependencies that exist when there is a relatively
fixed volume of water to be allocated. The best example
is non-rechargeable groundwater supplies. That stock resource should be rationally allocated over time, and one
party's use reduces the potential use of others and increases their costs.

Water quality interdependencies link closely to the
flow interdependencies but warrant added emphasis. Any
use of water changes its quality, possibly up but usually
down. The non-consumptive uses of instream water such as
hydro-electric generation and releases for navigation can
increase dissolved oxygen, usually a beneficial change;
but the water can become supersaturated with nitrogen, a
condition that kills fish. Municipal and industrial return flows always carry various pollutants, some of a bio-
degradable nature and others of a persistent type. Irri-

gation return flows carry pesticides, herbicides, fertilizers, and other dissolved salts. Some of these additions of pollutants are unplanned, but others intention-
ally use the water body as a waste sink. Naturally, all
subsequent users are affected.

The interdependencies mentioned above represent what
economists call externalities, i.e. physical linkages between the actions of one group and the productive potential of another group. Externalities are usually not
recognized by market processes because the connecting
water body is usually an unowned "open-access" resource,
i.e. free to those who care to use it. Even if the water
itself is clearly owned by specific parties, some of its
attributes may not be, especially its waste assimilative
capabilities. This lack of ownership means that "nobody's
property is everybody's property" and the resource is
heavily overused as a result.

There are many forms of market interdependency among
water users in a river basin. The industrial sector may
buy its raw materials from the agricultural, forestry, or
mining sectors, all of which use large quantities of
water in their processes. One irrigation project may
produce so much of some crop that its price is noticeably
depressed for all other existing or prospective irrigation projects. These are forms of pecuniary interdependencies, i.e. they are reflected in market transactions
and prices and private sector decision-makers can usually
be expected to anticipate them and take them into account.
However, public sector planners usually have to forecast
these reactions of the market to the creation of a new
project, such as anticipating the effect of a new irrigation project on the profitability of existing farms.

Complexity of river basin development

The easiest way to suggest the complexity of river
basin planning is to consider a small problem in arithme-
tic that represents the number of possible combinations
of projects that might constitute the development plan
for the basin. Consider a river basin with five reservoir sits, each having three possible types of development: no dam, small dam, or large dam. Without considering the variety of possible operating rules for each
reservoir, there are already $3^5 = 243$ possible configurations for development. If we allow two possible times at
which each reservoir might be constructed, then five possibilities exist at each site and the number of possibilities for the whole basin goes up to $5^5 = 3125$. If there
are five possible operating rules for each reservoir once
it is built, the number increases to $21^5 = 4$ million possible development and operating configurations.

In practice, no one can ever analyze each of these
possibilities in the attempt to identify the best plan,

but clearly some kind of project screening must be carried out systematically to avoid missing the best plan by
too wide a margin. This screening is sometimes carried
out with large-scale linear programming models[1] that
greatly simplify the hydrology and economics of the system but that permit ruling out a large portion of the development configurations, either on grounds of hydrologic
inconsistency or gross economic inefficiency. In the absence of formal modeling, skilled individuals must attempt the same exercise informally to avoid the situation
where one project, chosen early in the development of the
basin and quite attractive on its own merits, precludes a
highly desirable sequential development of the basin.

It seems unlikely that private agencies, frequently
concerned with single purposes like hydro-electric power,
would be motivated or able to carry out such analyses.

The complexity of river basin planning is greatly
increased by the necessity of considering non-structural
alternative ways of accomplishing the desired, objectives
of basin development. Regarding water supply, alternatives to expanding the supply system include demand management through pricing, restrictions, or rationing. In
flood control, alternatives to flood storage, canalizing
floodways, and building flood walls include floodplain
zoning, flood-proofing of structures, early warning systems, evacuation preparations, and post-flood relief capabilities. In addition to increasing the possible number
of development configurations, consideration of these
non-structural alternatives always requires a different
set of planning team skills. In addition to the usual
hydrologic, engineering, and economic skills, legal,
administrative, and social science (sociology, psychology,
anthropology) skills will be required.

Again, it seems unlikely that private agencies would
have the capabilities or the motivation to look at such a
wide range of alternatives.

Finally, the complexity of planning is increased by
the existence of substantial scale economies in the construction and operation of most types of water projects.
These scale economies relate both to the sheer size of
the project (e.g. capital costs per thousand cubic meters
of storage capacity usually fall as reservoir size increases) and to the incorporation of complementary multiple purposes in one project. For example, flood control
and irrigation water supply are highly complementary in
regions where stream flow is highly seasonal because of
snowmelt or monsoon rains.

Since some of the purposes of multiple-purpose projects relate to outputs for which the project authority
is unlikely to be able to collect any payments from beneficiaries (e.g. streamflow maintenance for fishlife, es-
thetics, and recreation, and possibly for flood control),
there is a high probability that private projects will

omit or undersize these purposes relative to what can be justified on the basis of social benefits and costs.

The existence of scale economies also raises problems regarding the possibility of economically efficient pricing of project outputs by private developers, a topic to be developed later in this chapter.

The need for flexibility in reallocating project outputs over time

Economic development results in a changing composition as well as level of economic activity, usually from a pattern of agriculture, forestry, fisheries, and mining to one increasingly dominated by manufacturing, services, and urbanized activities generally. At the same time, after the initial development of the best water sources in arid and semi-arid regions, the incremental costs of new supply development become extremely high. Table 1 illustrates the marginal costs of added reservoir storage for various regions of the United States.

Table 5.1
Long-run Marginal Storage Costs
for Western U.S. Water Development

Region	Cumulative Developed Supply (maf/yr.)	Marginal Storage Costs[a] (1970 dollars/acre-foot)
Lower Missouri	6 (1970 level)	–
	10	3.3
	12	6.9
Lower Arkansas	27 (1970 level)	–
	30	4.2
	45	5.4
Western Gulf	17 (1970 level)	–
	20	7.8
	22	11.7
	25	20.4
Central Pacific	29 (1970 level)	–
	42	8.7
	46	25.5
Pacific Northwest	70 (1970 level)	–
	120	4.2
	145	15.6
Upper Missouri Upper Arkansas Colorado Great Basin Rio Grande Southern Pacific	storage so intensively developed that additional storage will reduce total basin yields because of evaporative losses	

[a]The interest rate used in computing these costs was only 3.5 percent so the costs are understated.

Source: Charles W. Howe and K. William Easter, Interbasin Transfers of Water: Economic Issues and Impacts (Baltimore: Johns Hopkins University Press, 1971). Original data from Wollman and Bonem, The Outlook for Water (Baltimore: Johns Hopkins University Press, 1971).

At the same time that costs of new supply are becoming prohibitive, other economic changes may be lowering the value of water in some of its traditional uses, especially in irrigated agriculture. Kelso et al.[2] found that the direct cost (in incomes lost to agriculture) of a rational program of withdrawing 29 percent of the irrigation water being used in the Salt River Project (Arizona) was about $7 per thousand cubic meters, while the direct plus indirect income losses totalled about $12 per thousand cubic meters. Howe and Young[3] found that the state income foregone from abandoning certain inefficient irrigation areas in Colorado came to about $55 per thousand cubic meters. Gisser et al.[4] found that a rational transfer of 30 percent of the water consumed in irrigation in the common boundary area of Colorado, Arizona, New Mexico and Utah would result in direct and indirect regional income losses of $25 per thousand cubic meters. In each of these cases, the cost of developing new supplies would be several times these costs.

The social ownership of water and the use of multiple-objective planning in water development

The social ownership of water predominates throughout the world. Even in situations where relatively unrestricted private access to water is permitted, constraints on water quality and on interference with others' uses are always imposed in society's interest. Comparative studies of the institutional framework for water planning have classified modes of social ownership and control as follows:[5]

1. Central government ownership and control.
     Possible arrangements include:
     a. licensing of all surface and ground-
        water abstractions;
     b. issuance of limited life use contracts
        that are periodically renegotiated.
2. Cooperative control - provincial government
   ownership and control.
     Possible arrangements include:
     a. water bodies totally within a province
        are under provincial management, with
        inter-provincial and international
        bodies under central government;
     b. central government retains control only
        over navigation and international
        waters, including maritime fisheries.
3. Cooperative social ownership and control with qualified private access. This category is meant to include the systems of riparian law whereby private uses are permitted without formal licensing but wherein all detrimental externalities on other parties are presumably disallowed.

4. Modified private ownership. Under such systems, local traditions for the administration of water are allowed to prevail (e.g. farmers' associations allocating surface waters for irrigation), provided no contradictions to national interests (e.g. stoppage of navigation) arise. Water rights systems found in many semi-arid parts of the world fall into this category.

The point is that some degree of social control is always maintained. This follows partly from the need to control negative externalities but also from the desire to use water development and allocation as tools for achieving varied social objectives. Out of the latter has grown the beginnings of multiple-objective planning.

Many countries of the world have adopted an explicit framework of multiple objectives by which development projects are to be evaluated[6]. Among the so-called objectives (goals) are the traditional net economic benefits, environmental quality, regional development benefits, improvements in human health and safety, national self-sufficiency, etc. Naturally some of these objectives can be quantified and weighted in ways that permit their inclusion in the traditional economic net benefit analysis (e.g. shadow-pricing of labor, foreign exchange, etc.). Other objectives, such as environmental quality and various social objectives, defy expression in monetary values if not in physical terms.

The movement toward the explicit use of various objectives and away from apparent dependence on traditional economic efficiency analysis has been motivated by:[7]

> ...a general dissatisfaction with the project-by project application of rather traditional benefit-cost analysis in developing countries. Part of this dissatisfaction arises from the fact that a single metric - the benefit/cost ratio or present valued net benefits - often conceals more than it reveals about the full range of impacts arising from one or more projects...

If river basin and project plans are to be evaluated according to several objectives some of which represent non-appropriable public good benefits (flood control, public health, aesthetics, preservation concerns), basin plans and project designs cannot be left as private responsibilities. There must be an iterative process of communication between technical planners and politically responsible decision-makers who know what weights are appropriate.

Likely patterns of unplanned river basin development in semi-arid regions

Many of the world's low income regions are semi-arid or arid, areas where water is truly a scarce resource. The early stages of development of such regions always involve irrigated agriculture. Unfortunately, the natural pattern of unregulated development in semi-arid river basins involves large inefficiencies that may be difficult to overcome.

This pattern typically involves initial development of the bottomlands in the lower valley ahead of other areas for obvious reasons: better soils, flatter land contours, proximity to other settlements, ease of transportation, access to public utilities, etc. As population and cultivated areas expand, the lands higher in the valley are brought under irrigation. These later divisions begin to interfere with the use of water on the better lands further down, an obvious inefficiency.

If there is no system of water law that grants priority to the diversions of the older users, those parties will be motivated to build reservoir capacity to capture off-season flows so the diminished river flow can be augmented during the irrigation season. Unfortunately, it is much more advantageous to construct reservoir capacity higher in the basin: higher reservoirs command a larger area and permit the multiple use of return flows. Again, the unregulated pattern of development is likely to incorporate these additional inefficient features.

In addition to mutual interference with streamflows and poor placement of reservoir capacity, privately developed reservoirs, canals, and drains are likely to be uneconomically small because of failure to anticipate future development and settlement by others, including municipal development. The privately constructed works are likely to be single-purpose, too, when the inclusion of other functions, especially flood control and power generation, may well be economically desirable from the basin-wide point of view.

Finally, in addition to physical development, the process of institutional development may involve inefficiencies. Some traditional ways of allocating water tie it to the lands originally irrigated, thus preventing later transfers to new activities. This can be true of public agency water contracts, too.

All of these rather unique features of water resource systems, especially within a river basin context, indicate that a planning and coordinating role for the public sector is essential to efficient water development, as is the existence of a well defined legal framework. As we will see in a later section, there are also functions that can best be carried out by private water users, perhaps working in various cooperative modes.

SOME TECHNICAL ASPECTS OF RIVER SYSTEMS

While this chapter is devoted primarily to the institutional framework for the development and allocation of water, there are certain technical aspects of river development that should be understood by everyone interested in water policy. The following materials will be familiar to all technically trained readers but represent a worthwhile background for persons approaching the field from other disciplines.

Water occurs both as a stock and as a flow. Streams or overland runoff from precipitation find their ways into lakes, reservoirs, or the oceans. Groundwater exists as a stock, usually subject to flows of recharge. An important characteristic of water flows is that they are stochastic, that is, they are governed by physical processes that are best described as probabilistic. All naturally occurring water flows are therefore described by probability distributions and not simply by one number such as the average rate of flow.

The stochastic nature of flows is directly attributable to the nature of the physical systems generating them such as the accumulation and melting of mountain snows, the occurrence of precipitation and its infiltration into the soil and subsoil, and so on. These processes are subject to many influences that cannot be predicted with the current state of meteorology and related sciences, but it is often possible to quantify the resultant probability distribution of flows. Decisions on system development and related water-using activities are then based on these probability distributions. Water projects are intended to modify or transform the probability distributions of stream flows into patterns more useful (or less harmful) to man. Reservoirs and flood control works are the prime examples.

If a river has a uniform natural flow over time, then it provides a highly reliable supply for withdrawal or consumptive uses. If withdrawals are largely noncomsumptive and are returned to the stream, the waters can be used repeatedly. Total withdrawals could exceed the flow rate of the river. Consumptive uses are, of course, bounded by the flow of the river. The hydrograph of a large river in a high rainfall region is shown in Figure 2.

Reservoirs perform the regulating function of transforming uneven river flows into a more uniform pattern of withdrawals. To get a feeling for the process, imagine a perfectly regular, deterministic flow pattern for an unregulated river as shown in Figure 3. Superimposed on the diagram is a desired uniform rate of water withdrawal, w. What volume of storage (say in acre-feet) will be re-

Figure 5.2

The Annual Hydrograph of a River

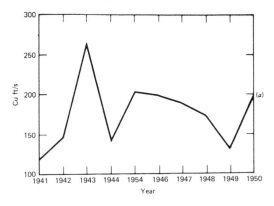

Figure 5.3

River Flows and Withdrawals

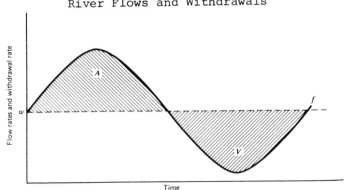

quired to permit this rate of withdrawal? Naturally, if
the flow curve f is always above the desired rate of
withdrawal, w, then no storage would be required. Water
could simply be diverted directly from the river. As
shown in the figure, however, there is a season each year
when desired withdrawal rates exceed flow, requiring the
storage of water during high flows for release during low
flows. The total required storage volume would be V,
provided that $V \leq A$. Since the data for such an analysis
come from the historical record of streamflow, there is,
of course, no guarantee that the record will be repeated.
The modern science of hydrology has grown out of the
study of the probability characteristics of water flows to
permit more adequate handling of problems of this type.

Water tends to be quite unevenly distributed in space and time. <u>Runoff</u> represents the quantity or flow rate of water that actually reaches streams or other water bodies. It therefore measures the maximum amount of water available for capture and control, although it does not include precipitation that percolates into the surface to be evaporated or transpired by plants.

Regions that have very little precipitation or runoff may still have large water supplies, either in the form of groundwater or from rivers flowing in from other regions of origin. Regions of sparse rainfall also experience highly variable rainfall and runoff.

Clearly, the more variable the inflow rate, the more storage will be required for a desired rate of withdrawal, especially when the inflows show strong positive serial correlations over time. It is also clear that any river will, for practical purposes, have a maximum uniform withdrawal rate. The maximum uniform withdrawal rate (ignoring evaporation losses) would be the mean flow rate of the stream. To achieve this rate would require huge volumes of storage, since some water might have to be carried over many years from some rare incident of extremely high flow to an interval of unusually low flow. In practice, because of evaporation losses, it is not physically possible to achieve a "yield" equalling the mean flow. As higher reliable yields are desired, the required volume of storage rises disproportionately. This is best seen in so-called "storage-yield curves" for particular rivers such as the Upper Missouri--see Figure 4. Note that, while the theoretical yield can approach the mean flow, the practical net yield reaches a maximum of about 23 billion gallons per day with storage of 70 million acre-feet. If storage exceeds this volume, evaporation losses exceed the amount of any added carryover.

Also note that several curves are shown, each with a specified chance of deficiency, that is, a probability that the system really will not permit the indicated level of withdrawal in any year. These probabilities are not zero because there is no theoretical upper bound to the length of low flow periods. These probabilities are, in practice, estimated by computer simulations of river flows with varying volumes of storage.

Given the storage-yield curves for a particular river, knowledge of potential dam sites permits estimating the costs of providing varying volumes of storage. The costs are partly for dam construction and partly for land and other resources that will be lost to the reservoir. If these costs are expressed on an annual basis the average and marginal costs of water supply at the storage site (with a specified level of reliability) can be computed. Such cost curves are shown for the upper Missouri Basin in Figure 5.

Once surface water is provided at the storage site,

Figure 5.4

Storage Required in the Upper Missouri Basin

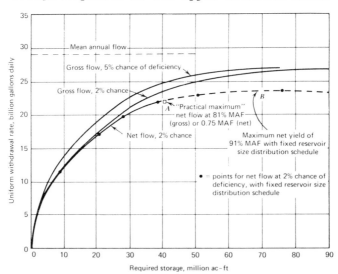

it must be transported to the areas of use. In speaking
of use, we must distinguish withdrawal rates and consumptive rates. Water diverted for once-through cooling of a
thermal-electric plant may be returned totally to the
stream (although at an elevated temperature that will increase evaporation), while water diverted for city use
may be one third consumed, the rest possibly being returned to the water source (usually degraded in quality).
Water diverted for the irrigation of crops may be almost
fully consumed, being lost through evaporation, transpir-
ation from plants, and perhaps being caught in aquifers
that do not return it to the stream.

Where the diversions are not fully consumed, the return flows can be very important to subsequent users,
making it possible to withdraw far more from a river than
its actual flow. Suppose a quantity W is withdrawn and
that the initial user consumes a fraction c, returning
$(1 - c)$ W to the stream. As subsequent users withdraw
that quantity in turn, consuming a fraction c, and so on,
the following total quantity of withdrawals is generated:

$$TW = W + (1 - c)W + (1 - c)^2 + \ldots + (1 - c)^{n-1}W$$

Figure 5.5

Total Annual and Marginal Costs of Added Water
Supply at the Storage Site, Upper Missouri Basin

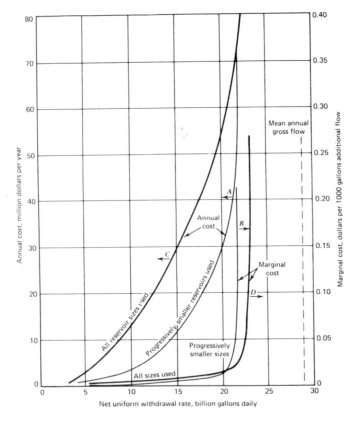

As the number of sequential users becomes large, this can
be approximated by

$$TW = \frac{W}{c}$$

This is referred to as the "return flow multiplier."

ESTABLISHING PROPERTY RIGHTS AND MARKETS IN WATER

The essential nature of the public sector's role in
water planning and at least coordinating project developments based on that planning has already been discussed
at length. Most countries go farther by including the

construction and operation of all large projects among
public sector functions. Unfortunately, public planning,
construction, and operation of projects is not a guarantee of social efficiency in the multiple-objective sense.
Public agencies develop biases over time and often become
captives of the groups they serve or of "empire building"
inclinations.[8]

Private decision-making can play an important role
in socially efficient water decisions even though it may
have to be guided by certain administrative or legal constraints. Consider a simple but very important real life
example. The island of Oahu in Hawaii is experiencing
rapid economic change: Honolulu, the capital city, is
growing, the tourist industry is booming, while agriculture and the Pearl Harbor Navy Base remain important activities and large users of water. The major source of
water is the Pearl Harbor aquifer, a large lens of fresh
water recharged by surface infiltration and situated on
top of saline aquifers. If withdrawals exceed freshwater
recharge for a very long period, intermixing of saline
and fresh water will occur, perhaps permanently impairing
the usefulness of the aquifer. Thus the available water
supply is definitely limited to a highly predictable
quantity per year.

How should the available water be allocated among
competing uses in the face of rapid economic change? Two
major systems have been proposed:
    1. the periodic issuance of licenses by a water
regulatory board;
    2. the establishment of saleable permits.

The main issues with the first proposal are to whom
the licenses should be issued and for what period the
licenses should remain valid. How are the water demands
of traditional sugar cane plantations to be balanced a-
gainst proposals for new tourist complexes? The problem
is that no regulatory board is likely to have the information needed to decide these issues. Further, the lim-
ited-life license establishes uncertainly regarding re-
newal that may discourage highly desirable long-lived investments.

Saleable permits would help overcome these problems
to some extent. A market or brokerage arrangement would
establish a market value for permits. Prospective activities could use the water prices thus established to
determine the feasibility of their activity and would not
have to fear non-renewal of the permits. Existing users
could decide whether or not to sell all or part of their
permits by comparing the price of permits to the profitability of water use at the margin. Even in the absence
of markets for water, the sugar plantations are turning
to sprinkler application in anticipation of some form of
water rationing.

An important feature of the Oahu case very much

favors the saleable permit arrangement: there are prac-
tically no third party or return flow effects in this
system. As we will soon see, this greatly enhances the
use of private market arrangements.

A potential problem with the private purchase and
sale of permits even under these ideal conditions is that
non-economic objectives may be ignored. In the context
of multiple-objective planning, aesthetic aspects or the
desire to maintain certain levels of agriculture or to
limit the extent of tourist activity may be important
social objectives. The most profitable uses of water may
not be consistent with these objectives. The fact that
these additional social values are not reflected in private profit calculus is just another form of externality
or third party effect. Whenever important externalities
are present, market processes cannot work well (although
they may still work better than alternative arrangements).

A reasonable compromise between the two systems that
would still be more efficient than a regulatory system
would be to allow saleable permits, subject to a well
publicized merit-point system that would reflect contemporary non-economic values. Such systems have worked well
in the housing market where limited numbers of construction permits have been allocated on the basis of points
awarded to aesthetics, open space, land contributed for
parks, provision of low-income units, etc.

Perhaps this example suggests three major advantages
the incorporation of private market processes brings to
water systems:

1. informational advantages in the form of the detailed knowledge of particular water use opportunities
held by individual entrepreneurs;

2. flexibility in the pattern of water use over
time as the mix and relative importance of different activities change;

3. a continual publicizing of the opportunity cost
of water in the form of its market price, motivating
users to select only economically justifiable uses.

The establishment of property rights in water

In water plentiful regions, the major concern is
likely to be protection against undue pollution by other
water users. The legal doctrine carried over from British Common Law is sometimes called the "riparian doctrine"
and it permits land owners fronting on water bodies to
withdraw water for use as long as they don't "greatly im-
pair" the quantity or quality. Since the major uses in
water plentiful regions are likely to be largely non-consumptive, the law, in effect, aims at water quality regulation.

In arid regions, water withdrawals, especially irrigation, are more likely to be highly consumptive. The

riparian doctrine does not fit such situations, so other legal systems for the governance of water have been developed for such regions. These other systems permit the ownership of water by users, usually in the form of a system of rights to use the water. Such water rights systems can usefully be compared in terms of the following important characteristics:

1. whether or not the rights have priorities associated with them that indicate the order in which the rights owners can demand water;

2. the extent to which the rights are transferable or saleable to other parties;

3. whether the quantification of a right is in terms of a volume of water per unit time (e.g. so many thousands of cubic meters per year) or in terms of a flow rate (e.g. so many cubic meters per second).

Our primary concern here will be to investigate item (1), namely the differences between priority rights systems and proportionate rights systems, the latter meaning that all shares represent a constant fraction of whatever water is available to the system. Item (2) will be discussed for each case, since without transferability there can be no markets. The real issue is the level of transactions costs associated with transfers.

The third characteristic above - volumes or flow rates - is being resolved in practice in favor of volumetric specification. In the United States, the more progressive state systems have re-defined the earlier "flow rights" in terms of annual volumes. This makes the total claims of each owner clear, in contrast to a flow rate that may be used a varying fraction of the time. This makes water system management much easier.

We now turn to analyses of some characteristics of priority and proportionate rights systems.

Priority rights systems

The priority water rights systems used by various western states in the U.S. (and found in numerous other countries) originated in the mountain mining areas where water was quite limited relative to land and other potential uses. Established users frequently found their stream flow stopped or diminished by the establishment of a new mining operation upstream. To avoid gunfights, a system of priorities based on the date of establishment of each use was created, restricting each use to the diversion rate and the return flow pattern that had been established. Each river came to have such a set of priority rights, and these rights were finally incorporated into state law. Priorities need not be related to the date of first use. Where no water rights system has existed, it should be perfectly possible to create a set of rights in standard volumetric units (e.g. 10^3 m^3), with

112

certain classes of rights having higher priorities, i.e.
first call on available water.

The functioning of a priority system depends on the
probability distribution of seasonal water availability.
The senior rights have a high probability of getting
their water every season while the junior rights have
lower probabilities of receiving their entitlements. If
the quantities of water associated with each right are
labeled r_1, r_2, ..., r_n,... in decending order of priority, Figure 6 gives a visual picture of the probabilities
involved.

Figure 5.6

Probabilities Associated With
A Priority Rights System

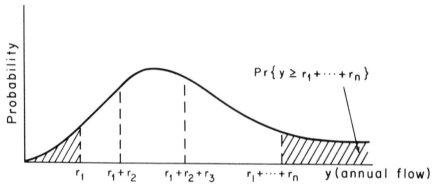

The curve represents the probability density function of annual river flows. Thus, an area under the
curve represents a probability. For example, if r_1 is
the annual quantity that can be claimed by the most senior
right, the area under the curve to the left of r_1 is the
probability that the annual flow will be less than this
most senior right. The area under the right tail of the
curve to the right of $(r_1 + \ldots + r_n)$ is the probability
that the total flow will be at least great enough to satisfy the n highest priority rights. It is easy to see
that the degree of assurance of water availability increases with the seniority of the right held.

The <u>economic efficiency</u> argument favoring priority
rights is that certain uses require the assurance of a
highly reliable supply of water before it becomes worthwhile to invest in the production process. For example,
a food-processing plant or a citrus orchard would not be
feasible if the water supply failed frequently. Other
water using activities such as the growing of grains or
mining operations may not be subject to much damage from

variations in water supply. The former activities would
presumably find it worthwhile to buy high priority (or
"senior") rights, while the latter might find low priority ("junior") rights quite acceptable.

This is illustrated in Figure 7 where the demand
functions for water withdrawals by two users are shown.
For simplicity, we assume that each user would withdraw
the same amount of water when water is plentiful, Q_0.
When the total amount available is less than $2Q_0$, someone
has to reduce their water use. If the reduction were imposed on User 1 (D_1), the losses would be much greater
than if the reduction were imposed on User 2 (D_2).

Figure 5.7

Demands for Water and
the Allocation of Shortages

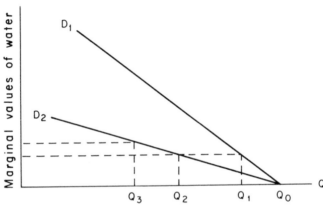

While such a system may provide the highly reliable
water supplies needed by some classes of users, there are
disadvantages in the form of short-term inefficiencies in
the allocation among the users. If we assume away the
complexities associated with return-flows and differing
consumptive fractions, short-term efficiency requires
that the marginal values of water be the same for both
users. Maintaining this condition requires that User 1
and User 2 share any shortage that occurs when total
water availability is less than $2Q_0$. This is illustrated
by the points Q_1 and Q_2 when $Q_1 + Q_2$ is the total supply.
However, a strict priority system would permit User 1 to
keep using Q_0 while all shortages would be absorbed by
User 2 at Q_3.

Priority systems need not be administered in such a
strict fashion. Senior rights holders may be allowed to
sell part of their water on a short-term basis without
losing title to it, provided the sale does not injure
other water users. When there are only a few rights

owners on a stream, bargaining may result in efficient
short-term sales of this sort. This has been observed
frequently in Colorado.[9] In Figure 7, with the prospective allocation being Q_0 to the senior and Q_3 to the junior, the junior's marginal value exceeds that of the senior, indicating that bargaining a different split of the
water could be advantageous to both.

Proportionate rights systems

A proportionate rights system is one in which each
share permits its owner to claim a proportionate share of
the water available in given year. If a water conservancy district having management control over a river basin creates 1000 ownership rights in the district, each
right would be entitled to 1/1000 of the water in the
river each year. Obviously, the more variable the river
flow, the more variable the amount that can be claimed by
any share. Thus, this system is a "share-alike" system.
No right has priority over others. Let's investigate
some of the properties of such a system. The following
relationships are useful in picturing this system:

N ≡ number of rights issued.

n_i ≡ number of rights held by owner i.

Q ≡ total amount of water available in a given year or season, a random variable.

Q_i ≡ $(\frac{n_i}{N})Q$ ≡ the amount that can be claimed by member i.

μ_Q ≡ the mean (average) streamflow.

μ_{Q_i} ≡ $(\frac{n_i}{N})\mu_Q$ ≡ the mean amount of water that can be claimed by user i.

σ_Q ≡ standard deviation of flows in the river.

σ_{Q_i} ≡ $(\frac{n_i}{N})\sigma_Q$ ≡ standard deviation of the quantity that can be claimed by user i.

Under this system, a rights owner's supply is increased
by buying more rights. On the average, the owner gets
his/her proportionate part of the mean flow available to
the district, μ_Q. However, as the number of rights owned
increases, both the owner's mean supply and the variabil-
ity of that supply (as measured by the standard deviation)
increase proportionately (see above). The situation of
the rights owner is depicted in Figure 8.

Obviously, if the rights owner needs to "guarantee"
a particular quantity, Q_D, he can increase the probability of getting Q_D by buying more rights, up to the point
where he owns all the rights. At that point, his probability distribution is that of the entire system. In
most cases, he cannot actually guarantee Q_D unless there

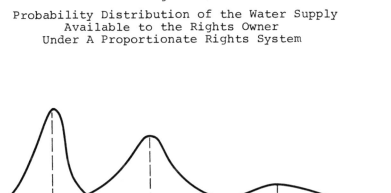

Figure 5.8

Probability Distribution of the Water Supply
Available to the Rights Owner
Under A Proportionate Rights System

is a minimum flow level that exceeds Q_D.

What are the <u>advantages</u> of this system? The first
stems from the <u>homogeneity</u> of the rights. All rights are
interchangeable and that makes establishment of an efficient market much easier than is the case with priority
rights where each right is unique.

A second advantage vis-à-vis the priority rights
system develops when the various water users have similar
water demand (benefit) functions. They would be expected
to hold similar numbers of rights (allowing some variation for risk aversion), so the available water would be
divided evenly among them. Again ignoring return flows
and possibly different consumptive fractions, this equal
division of water guarantees approximate equality of
marginal values of water among users.

Thus it appears that priority rights systems have
distinct efficiency advantages when users' demand functions are quite different, while proportionate rights
systems have efficiency advantages when users' demand
functions are similar. Demand functions are likely to be
similar in areas devoted primarily to a homogeneous type
of agriculture.

A final question about the proportionate rights system is that of achieving greater reliability of water
supply for activities that are sensitive to water supply
fluctuations. Greater reliability can be achieved by
buying additional shares until the probability of shortage is reduced to an acceptable level. As an example,
assume that each share has an expected annual claim of
1000 m³ with a standard deviation of 200 m³. A particular business requires an annual amount of 10,000 m³ with

95 percent reliability. Since $\mu_i = 1000n_i$ and $\sigma_i = 200n_i$, the number of shares held, n_i, can be increased until the probability of a supply of less than 10,000 m^3 is reduced to 0.05. If annual flows were normally distributed (which they clearly are not), this would require the purchase of 15 shares which would have a mean yield of 15,000 m^3 and would yield at least 10,000 m^3 with probability = 0.95. This is illustrated in Figure 9.

Figure 5.9

Guaranteeing 10,000 m^3 with 95% Reliability
in A Proportionate Rights System

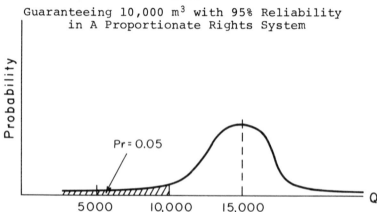

A major disadvantage of this system can be the in-efficient use or waste of the "excess water" held by a risk averter as in Figure 9. There the user holds rights to 15,000 m^3 on the average to guarantee receipt of 10,000 m^3 with high probability. What happens to this average excess of 5,000 m^3?

In most systems, this problem is recognized by allow-ing rights owners to sell their water temporarily--one season at a time--as they find they will have an excess. This occurs very frequently when cities hold excess rights to achieve reliability and then typically "rent" part of their water back to the agricultural sector. In these situations, there are actually two water markets: the market for permanent water rights and the season "rental" market.

Is this an economically efficient arrangement? Rent-al water is clearly subject to a greater degree of risk than water claimed by a rights holder. This affects the kinds of uses people will be willing to make of this water, directing the water toward crops that are less prone to damage by water shortage. These are generally the lower valued grain and forage crops. Thus, high risk aversion on the parts of cities (or industries) comes at the expense of reductions in the value of agricultural output.

The various characteristics we have discussed are summarized in Table 2.

Table 5.2

A Comparison of Some Characteristics of
Priority and Proportionate Rights Systems

	Priority Rights	Proportionate Rights
General advantage	different degrees of supply reliability can be purchased	rights are homogeneous, easier to establish market
General disadvantage	rights non-homogeneous, more difficult to organize market	differing degrees of reliability must be created by holding excess shares, with possible inefficient use of water
When users are alike	short-run inefficiencies during water shortages	efficient allocation among users during shortage
When users are not alike	prevents extreme loss to sensitive users during shortage but generates some short-term inefficiencies due to marginal products not being equal	either excessive losses to water sensitive users during shortage or potentially inefficient use due to risk hedging
When water supply is highly variable	protects sensitive investments but results in some short-term inefficiencies	makes protection of sensitive investments difficult but equates marginal values where users are alike

The continuing problem of third party effects through return flows.

The preceding discussion was based on the simplifying assumption that return flows weren't very important. While return flows were discussed briefly under the technical aspects of river systems, that discussion greatly understated their importance and the complexity they add to the establishment of economically efficient water markets. Figure 10 illustrates a special case.

We assume that the total flow is divided into two branch flows, W_1 and W_2, the first of which is totally diverted by User A and the second by User C. Suppose that A and C compare marginal water values and that

Figure 5.10

A Hypothetical Canal System
With Four Water Users

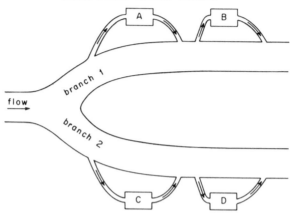

$MV(W_1) > MV(W_2)$. This sets up a privately profitable
water sale since A can profitably buy some of C's water.

This sale seems desirable if we ignore the return
flows. Suppose the legal system permits sales without
consideration of return flows. Then User D will suffer
losses and User B will gain. Naturally, if B's gains exceed D's losses, the return flow effects strengthen the
case for transferring water from C to A. If B's gains
are less than D's losses, then the sale is less attractive or perhaps shouldn't be undertaken at all.

What conditions would be required to guarantee that
free market sales would always lead to greater efficiency?

1. The exact nature of the return flows would have
to be known.
2. The seller would have to be required to pay for
any damages downstream, while the buyer would have to be
able to sell the added return flow created by his purchase.

The technical difficulties in determining the pattern of
return flows are evidenced by the extended court battles
that sometimes occur over proposed transfers, with expert
hydrologists on each side presenting quite different estimates. Regarding condition (2), most legal systems go
only part of the way: they make the seller liable for
damages to downstream parties, but they prohibit the buyer from claiming the right to sell his return flow.[10]

Many legal systems act to protect downstream parties
who have been using the return flow from any damage what-
soever. Then a highly beneficial sale of water, say from

User C to User A, might be precluded altogether, just because of minor damages to D. More frequently, because of the great uncertainty regarding the extent and timing of actual return flows, the water courts will proceed on the assumption that if C's actual transfer to A is restricted to what C was consumptively using before, then D will not be damaged. Thus, C sells his entire water right but only part get transferred to A. The rest must remain in C's branch canal to protect D against loss.

Naturally, these legal protections for downstream parties have grown out of concern for equity rather than efficiency, so they frequently are overly protective of downstream parties.

One situation in which return flow effects are allowed to be ignored under some legal systems occurs when a water project brings new water into a basin through trans-basin diversion facilities. The agency having title to the new water may claim ownership of the new return flows, too, and could, in theory, attempt to use or sell not only the initial volume brought in, but also the return flows. Again, however, the uncertainty of these return flows co-mingled with pre-existing streamflows makes such claims almost impossible to enforce. At best, the agency allocating the water gets to ignore the return flows and is freer to reallocate first uses of the water among users. Under these circumstances, the efficiency question is whether or not the increased flexibility of transferring the first use is worth more than the possible net losses to third parties.[11]

THE PRICING OF WATER FROM PUBLIC PROJECTS AND RELATED LAND TAX ISSUES

Consider a publicly constructed water project providing water supply. What do we mean by the price of water from the project? In economics, price always means the charge per unit of output that accompanies transfer of output from supplier to user. In more common usage, "price" may refer to financing arrangements of a broader nature and, in fact, it may be more difficult to determine just what the price of water means. Consider the following fairly typical example.

1. A public water agency constructs a water supply project. The agency operates the project but contracts with a water district for the sale of the total project supply.
2. The district agrees to repay the agency for all operating costs and to repay the capital costs according to an agreed-upon schedule.
3. The district develops a mechanism to determine who will get the water. The district then levies one or more of the following charges:

a. a fixed charge per year per user;
b. a price per unit of water delivered;
c. a tax, usually based on land, that is
levied either against all irrigated land in the
district or against all land (including towns) in
the district.
4. If the water, once issued to users, is readily
transferable, a market for water may come into existence.
The necessary condition for existence of this market is
that the marginal value of water to some users exceeds
the charges of types (a) and (b) above. Then, if transactions costs aren't too high, trading will be worthwhile.

What is the price of water under these fairly typical
circumstances? In common parlance, it could refer to the
agency's charges against the user (a and b above) and/
or the market price that becomes established for transferable water. If water is plentiful, the scarcity value
reflected in the market may be very low, but as demand
for water grows, the scarcity element reflected in the
market price may come to dominate all others.
An example is found in the Northern Colorado Water
Conservancy District that has contracted with the U.S.
Bureau of Reclamation for the purchase of all water from
a large trans-mountain diversion project. The District
is repaying the capital costs according to an agreed upon
schedule and pays the operating costs of the project that
is operated by the Bureau. In turn, the District has
issued 310,000 "shares" that entitle the holder to delivery of 1/310,000th of the water delivered to the District every year. Each agricultural share owner is assessed $2.50 per share per year by the District. In ad-
dition, all real property owners within the District's
boundaries pay a small ad valorum tax on their properties
to the District, whether they are users of District-pro-
vided water or not. The justification for such a tax was
that all residents of the District benefit at least indirectly from the added water supply through higher levels
of economic activity. The $2.50 charge per share about
covers the District's annual operating costs, while the
tax proceeds are used to repay the capital costs to the
Bureau of Reclamation.
In this case, the shares are freely transferable and
two very active markets have developed:
1. a market for the permanent transfer of shares;and
2. a short-term "rental" market in which water is
temporarily made available to buyers without permanent
transfer of the shares.
Prices for permanent transfers of shares have risen to
$1800 while rental prices vary within and between seasons
from $8 per 10^3m^3 to about $32 per 10^3m^3, depending on
climate conditions. In contrast, when the shares were

first issued in the 1955-57 period, it was difficult to
give all of them away!

What is the relevant price to the user in this case?
If the user "rents" water from a permanent owner, the
going rental price is all that's relevant. If the user
needs an assured supply and buys a permanent share that
entitles him to approximatly $10^3 m^3$ of water, the relevant
price consists of the annual service charge by the District of $2.50 plus interest on the investment in the
share, say 10 percent of $1800, a total of $182.50 per
$10^3 m^3$.

Thus, the concept of the relevant price is not as
simple in water systems as it is in the retail market for
food. The relevant price may be comprised of several
parts as illustrated above.

Not withstanding the possible complexity in the meaning of price, the charges that vary with quantity of water
used perform important economic and financial roles that
are discussed in the next section.

A few comments on the use of land taxes are warranted
first. Land taxes may be of two types: those levied
against all lands, whether served by the water supply or
not; and those levied just against the lands directly
served by the project. A land tax of either type is often
considered a desirable revenue source for a water agency
because it provides a stable, predictable revenue. When
an agency depends only on the direct price of water to
the user as a source of revenue, the agency frequently
finds that its revenues fall sharply during droughts,
just when they may have to incur added costs to provide
emergency supplies or repair leaks from the system. Naturally, this result assumes that the price charged doesn't
vary with water scarcity, but administered agency prices
seldom do.

If the tax is levied against all lands, served or not,
then it won't affect the water user's production decisions
concerning the mixes of land, labor, and capital used,
provided it isn't high enough to make activities finan-
cially infeasible. However, if the tax is levied just a-
gainst served lands, it increases the effective cost of
land to the user and biases his decision in favor of less
land intensive technologies. Since the tax generally is
not linked to costs that vary with the extent of land
used, it doesn't represent a real cost to society. Thus,
the bias against land use is inefficient and undesirable.

Developing countries have frequently used land taxes
to penalize or discourage the accumulation of large hold-
ings of inactive land. The necessity of paying an annual
tax stimulates the owner to plan some revenue producing
activity to help cover the tax. If the tax is levied a-
gainst all lands, it will not bias the selection of production methods, but if it is levied only against, say,
irrigated lands, then it will unduly bias the choice of

land-water combinations against the land input.

PRICING PROJECT OUTPUTS: FINANCIAL AND ECONOMIC EFFICIENCY ROLES OF PRICES

The pricing of project outputs is very heavily empha-sized in economic analysis and a very elaborate litera-ture on efficient pricing of publicly provided goods has developed.[12] The traditional roles that project output prices are expected to play are:

1. to ration efficiently the available supply among users;

2. to reflect the real long term costs of providing the output so that investment decisions in industries that use the product or service as an input will be based on correct cost information;

3. to signal when additional capacity is justified for the production of the output itself;

4. to provide funds to the project agency for con-tinued project operation and maintenance;

5. to attain certain equity objectives.

In practice, public sector agencies pay much less at-tention to pricing than economic theory or the literature would suggest. Why? Certainly one reason is that there are conflicts among the various roles that prices are supposed to play.

Let us illustrate some of these conflicts. The ef-ficient allocation of output role requires <u>flexible</u> prices. In the very short run (seasonally or even daily) there is the problem of peak demands. In the intermed-iate term when project capacity is fixed, there is the problem of efficient utilization of capacity. Figure 11 illustrates the role price is supposed to play in the in-termediate term.

Figure 5.11

Efficient Pricing of Project Output
in the Intermediate Term

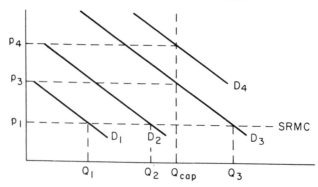

Given the capacity of the project Q_{cap}, and the level
of short run marginal costs, SRMC, it is economically efficient to supply the output to any user to whom the value
exceeds SRMC. In period 1 when demand conditions are
represented by the demand curve D_1, the quantity Q_1 should
be produced. Efficient production in period 2 is determined the same way. When project capacity is reached,
the available output, Q_{cap}, must be rationed among users.
Price is the <u>efficient</u> way of rationing, e.g. p_3 in period
3 and p_4 in period 4.

What is meant by the <u>efficient</u> way of rationing? Suppose capacity has been reached in Figure 11, e.g. in period 3. At p_3 only those users whose willingness-to-pay
is in excess of p_3 will opt to buy the output. Supply
and demand match. Suppose, however, that price were kept
at p_1. There would be an excess demand per period in the
amount $Q_3 - Q_{cap}$. Some form of rationing would be required, perhaps long queues, a lottery, social privilege,
or knowing the right people. Whatever non-price method
is used, some users who place only a low value on the
output will end up getting part of the supply while some
high-value users will be excluded. Maximum economic benefits from Q_{cap} will not be achieved.

Price flexibility conflicts with other functions of
price. Suppose a factory that uses large volumes of water
as an input observes that the price of water is p_1. It
then decides to install water-intensive technology. Later,
water price rises and the factory may be in financial difficulty. It has chosen an inappropriate technology.

Financial and equity objectives may not be well served by flexible prices. They make the prediction of revenues difficult and may place water supply agencies in
financial jeopardy as we have seen. Individuals and firms
that were established in the region when water costs were
low find themselves injured by rising prices.

Thus, in practice, it appears that prices cannot be
highly flexible. However, the use of a <u>price</u> (rate)
<u>schedule</u> that is known to all users is not precluded. A
price schedule permits water users to calculate their
future water costs but also can present them with information on various dimensions of real costs. A price
schedule can include the following dimensions:

1. a fixed charge per period to reflect costs that
don't vary with water used;

2. an increasing block structure in terms of total
water use per period, to reflect long-run increasing supply costs, yet not injure the small-scale user;

3. a seasonal shift of the block structure to reflect the shortages of raw water and/or supply system
capacity during the summer or dry season;

4. daily peak charges in highly sophisticated systems
such that price changes by time of day to alleviate problems of peak-hour use.

These remarks are sufficient to show that the determination of an optimal price schedule is a difficult task and is a matter of compromise among the various goals sought through pricing. However, project output price is an important element in project management. The intended pricing scheme must be consistent with project capacity, demand conditions, and financial requirements of the project. Some pricing arrangements are demonstrably inappropriate.

THE POSSIBLE ROLE OF INTER-BASIN TRANSFERS OF WATER

Our discussion thus far has emphasized the river basin as the natural unit for water management. There are, of course, many river basins that have very little water, and there are frequent cases where population and/ or good soils are found in different river basins from most of the water. Chile and Mexico are examples of the latter. Chile consists of a large number of short river basins running from the Andes Mountains to the Pacific Ocean. The northern basins contain some of the most arid lands on earth, but also some of the best soils. The central and southern basins have most of the water but poorer soils and shorter growing seasons. The river basin structure of the west coast of Mexico is very similar. These features have stimulated intense interest in transferring water from the wet to the dry basins. In the case of Chile, this could be accompanied by the generation of large net amounts of hydro-electric power because of the large altitude differences, while in Mexico large quantities of power would be required for pumping.[13]

The Soviet Union is planning the largest water transfers ever seriously considered, from the Ob River to Central Asia and perhaps as far east as the Volga, Don, Kuban, and Dnieper Basins.[14]

What unique issues are raised by interbasin transfers of water? The first is the energy intensity of most projects. Most interbasin transfers involve large pumping or tunneling requirements. Both are energy intensive and energy is increasingly costly. A full, objective assessment of present and future energy costs must be made. In the U.S., an important factor in the feasibility of large transfers was found to be the extent to which power recovery was possible.[15] If, after pumping, there is a large altitude drop to the points of use, the water can be passed through turbines with the recovery of a substantial part of the original pumping power. In a very few cases, net power generation may be possible, as in the Chilean case described earlier.

The second issue is the opportunity cost of water in the basins of origin. This seems an obvious point but often has been ignored in planning and assessment. Opportunity costs take the following forms:

1. present and future consumptive uses of water;
2. foregone hydro-electric energy generation;
3. negative impacts on fisheries;
4. poorer conditions for navigation;
5. deteriorated water quality.

Even if present opportunity costs are low because of a
low state of development in the basin of origin, the out-
ward transfer of water may preclude future developments
of importance.

A third issue is the timing of the project. The huge
cost of most water transfer projects makes the issue of
timing particularly important. If the need for the water
is 25 years in the future, there is no need to build the
project now. If local water supplies can satisfy growing
demands at lower costs, they should be utilized first.

The importance of the timing issue is well illustrated in a study by Cummings whose study of the Hermosillo
aquifer in Sonora, Mexico was linked to a larger study of
the desirability of large-scale interbasin transfers a-
long the west coast of Mexico.[16] His study indicated
that the most efficient pattern of development would be
the continued "mining" of the Hermosillo aquifer for a
period of nearly 30 years, after which the marginal values
of water in the Hermosillo Basin would have risen to
equality with the full cost of imported water. Partial
results of that study are shown in Table 3.

CONCLUSIONS: GENERAL POLICY IMPLICATIONS FOR THE ROLES
OF PUBLIC AND PRIVATE SECTORS

The points covered above imply rather unique roles
for both the public and private sectors. The public sector must develop a capability for river basin planning so
that it can, at a minimum, coordinate development activities in each basin to avoid serious externalities and inefficiencies. The economies of multiple-purpose projects
also imply that the public sector must participate in
project design so that potential project outputs of a
public, non-saleable nature (flood control, water quality,
fish and wildlife management, and aesthetics) are efficiently incorporated in project designs and operating rules.

Given the complexity of basin-wide coordination, it
may simply be easiest to let the public sector plan,
build projects, and supply raw water at the river-basin
level. The administrative arrangements for doing this
can take many forms, from central government ministries
to river basin commissions or agencies that are largely
governed by boards of directors chosen from the private
sector.

The private sector has unique functions to perform,
particularly in making the dynamic decisions about the
allocation of water to different uses. The raw water
supplied by public agencies can be sold to private parties

Table 5.3

Solution for the Optimum Rate of Groundwater Use and the Timing of Interbasin Imports in La Costa de Hermosillo, Mexico

Year	Annual rate of pumping (million m^3)	Groundwater storage at the beginning of year (million m^3)	Increase in storage attributable to pump relocation (million m^3)	Shadow value of water not discounted (dollars/m^3)	Increase in saltwater intrusion (km)
1	1,219.1	22,253.0	1,989.6	0.0008	0.96
2	1,219.1	23,023.6	795.3	0.0035	0.96
3	1,219.1	22,234.0	828.1	0.0038	0.96
4	1,219.1	21,412.0	829.4	0.0042	0.96
5	1,219.1	20,588.7	829.5	0.0046	0.96
6	1,219.1	19,765.3	829.5	0.0051	0.96
7	1,219.1	18,941.9	829.5	0.0054	0.96
8	1,219.1	18,118.5	829.5	0.0060	0.96
9	1,206.3	17,295.1	143.3	0.0067	0.95
10	1,206.3	17,834.8		0.0074	0.95
11	1,206.3	16,941.7		0.0080	0.95
12	1,206.3	16,048.6		0.0089	1.7
13	1,206.3	15,091.2		0.0096	1.7
14	1,218.6	13,976.3		0.0109	1.7
15	1,202.2	12,806.5		0.0118	1.7
16	1,126.5	11,638.3		0.0122	1.4
17	1,048.7	10,546.3		0.0124	1.4
18	978.5	9,552.7		0.0134	1.3
19	915.3	8,656.0		0.0138	1.3
20	865.1	7,848.5		0.0141	1.0
21	796.5	7,115.5		0.0156	0.9
22	756.7	6,471.1		0.0173	0.9
23	603.5	5,890.4		0.0175	0.5
24	555.3	5,480.2		0.0178	0.4
25	552.5	5,164.1		0.0184	0.4
26	527.0	4,876.2		0.0188	0.4
27	524.6	4,621.5		0.0192	0.4
28	512.5	4,378.2		0.0203	0.3
29	510.3	4,150.0		0.0224	0.3
30	508.1	3,928.0		0.0246	0.3
31	506.0	3,709.9		0.0272	0.3
32	503.9	3,495.1		0.0296	0.3
33	501.8	3,283.1		0.0320	0.3
34	500.0	3,074.1		0.0360	0.3
35	497.7	2,868.0		0.0360	0.3
36	350.0	2,644.5		0.0400	0.3

Source: Cummings, 1974, p. 98.

through systems of saleable water rights. The more easily transferable and divisible these shares, the more efficient will be the allocation of water over time.

Saleable water rights not only permit efficient reallocation among uses over time but <u>motivate</u> the efficient use of water by making the opportunity cost of water obvious to the user. Without some type of market for water, it has proven very difficult to motivate efficient water use, especially in agriculture.

Large-scale interbasin transfers are almost necessarily carried out by the public sector because of their profound hydrologic, environmental, economic, and social impacts over two or more river basins. The construction cost is likely to be so high and the risks so great that only the public sector could finance such projects. Continued operation will require attention to developing conditions in both the basin of origin and destination, a task considerably more extensive and difficult than most private interests and capabilities.

In closing, we note again that there are many alternative legal and administrative arrangements within which the public and private sectors can carry out those functions to which they are especially well adapted.

Footnotes

1. Jacoby, Henry D. and Daniel P. Loucks, "The Combined Use of Optimization and Simulation Models in River Basin Planning" in Richard de Neufville and David H. Marks (eds.) Systems Planning and Design, Englewood Cliffs, N.J.: Prentice-Hall, Inc. 1974.

2. Kelso, Maurice M., William E. Martin, and Lawrence E. Mack, Water Supplies and Economic Growth in An Arid Environment: An Arizona Case Study, Tucson: University of Arizona Press, 1973.

3. Howe, Charles W. and Jeffrey T. Young, "Indirect Economic Impacts from Salinity Damages in the Colorado River Basin" in Jay C. Andersen and Alan C. Kleinman (eds.) Salinity Management Options for the Colorado River, Report P-78-003, Utah Water Research Laboratory, Utah State University, Logan, Utah, June 1978, Table 7-4, Appendix 7.

4. Gisser, Micha et al., "Water Trade-off Between Electric Energy and Agriculture in the Four Corners Area," Water Resources Research, Vol. 15, No. 3, June 1979.

5. Howe, Charles W., "The Design and Evaluation of Institutional Arrangements for Water Planning and Management," paper prepared for the United Nations Water Conference, Mar del Plata, Argentina, 14-15 March 1977, E/CONF.70/A.4, 18 Nov. 1976.

6. U.S. Water Resources Council, "Principles and Standards for Water and Related Land Resources Planning: Level C," Federal Register, Part II, Monday, September 29, 1980, pp. 64366-64400.

7. Sfeir-Younis, Alfredo and Daniel W. Bromley, Decision-Making in Developing Countries: Multiobjective Formulation and Evaluation Methods, New York: Praeger Publishers, 1977, p. vii.

8. For excellent discussions of the types of biases that creep into public sector water development, see John V. Krutilla, "Is Public Intervention In Water Resources Development Conducive to Economic Efficiency?", Natural Resources Journal, January 1966; Robert A. Young, "Economic Analysis and Federal Irrigation Policy: A Reappraisal," Western Journal of Agricultural Economics, Vol. 3, No. 2, Dec. 1978.

9. See Howe, Charles W., et al. "Drought-Induced Problems and Responses of Small Towns and Rural Water Entities in Colorado: The 1976-1978 Drought," Completion Report No. 95, Colorado Water Resources Research Institute, Colorado State University, June 1980.

10. Under the law system known as "appropriations doctrine" in the western United States, all return flows

become "part of the stream" and can be claimed by rights
holders downstream. The water courts will also generally
act to prevent any damage to downstream parties.

11. These arrangements are found in the Northern
Colorado Water Conservancy District in Colorado, U.S.A.,
which is the distributing agency for the Colorado-Big
Thompson trans-mountain diversion project. Studies have
indicated that the gains from increased transferability
greatly offset any net third party losses. See Howe,
Charles W., Dennis R. Schurmeier, and William D. Shaw,Jr.,
Innovations in Water Management: An Ex-Post Analysis of
the Colorado-Big Thompson Project..., Resources for the
Future, Inc., forthcoming 1982.

12. See, for example, Selma Mushkin (ed.), Public
Prices for Public Products, Washington, D.C.: The Urban
Institute, 1972.

13. Garduño, Héctor, Eduardo Mestre, and Francisco
Tapia, "Large-Scale Transfers Within Master Water Planning in Mexico," Water Supply and Management, Vol.2,1978.

14. Voropaev, G. V., "The Scientific Principles of
Large Scale Areal Redistribution of Water Resources in
the U.S.S.R., Water Supply and Management, Vol.2, 1978.

15. Howe, Charles W. and K. William Easter, Interbasin Transfers of Water: Economic Issues and Impacts,
Baltimore: Johns Hopkins Press, 1971.

16. Cummings, Ronald G., Interbasin Water Transfers:
A Case Study in Mexico, Baltimore: Johns Hopkins Press,
1974.

6
Implementing Planning for Multiple Purpose Water Reclamation Projects in Developing Countries: Some Perspectives from the U.S. Experience

Ronald G. Cummings and H. Stuart Burness

INTRODUCTION

In an earlier paper in this volume,[1] Professor Howe's discussion of multiple purpose planning for water projects in developing countries stresses the importance of institutional frameworks and water pricing as they relate to plans for water resources development. An institutional framework determines, among other things, the rules to be followed in identifying and valuing benefits and costs to be included in measures for project efficiency (usually, a benefit-cost measure). The pricing of water relates to such things as efficient allocations of water and the distribution of water rents ("windfall benefits" a la Howe[2]). Generally, one would expect these two aspects to be interrelated; thus, water pricing, and the attendant allocation of water, would affect the nature of benefits and costs used in measures of project efficiency.

U.S. institutions related to irrigation water have undergone dramatic changes through time. As is developed below, one sees in the history of U.S. reclamation policy institutional principles which range from primary reliance on market criteria to the formal adoption of social accounting criteria. The substance of these changes, and reasons underlying these changes, bear directly on Howe's earlier discussions concerning the "necessary" role of the public sector in water resources development and may be of interest to planners in developing countries in their efforts to develop appropriate (to their cultural setting) institutional frameworks for analyses of water projects.

Further, water pricing policies have changed over time in the U.S. One dimension of these policies which may be of particular interest to the planner in a developing country concerns the magnitude of subsidies, primarily to irrigated agriculture, implicit in a water pricing - repayment policy. Ideally, if subsidies are to be given to a particular sector, the level of such subsidies should be easily identified inasmuch as this datum may be an important input to the decision making process for public

investments. As is developed below, practices followed
in the U.S. for cost allocation and related water pricing
have had the effect of obscuring the level of subsidies
(if any) enjoyed by the agricultural sector. Appreciation of the nature of these practices may then be useful
to planners in developing countries in forming assessment
procedures which, first, result in precise measures for
any subsidy granted to any economic sector and, second,
avoid the many times acrimonious debates surrounding the
existence and non-existence of subsidies which have often
arisen in the consideration of water project investments
in the U.S.

To the end of developing these arguments in section two
a sketch is given of the history of U.S. reclamation policy; primary attention in this section is given to institutional settings for water planning in the U.S., how
such institutions changed over time and the impacts of
such changes on methods used to assess the social efficiency of water projects. In section three attention is
turned to water pricing policies and related issues concerning the allocation of project costs between project
features as they relate to subsidies. Here we show that
practices used by U.S. agencies for the allocation of
project costs tend to overstate the level of any subsidy
to irrigated agriculture and that methods used in imple-
menting water pricing policies have the effect of totally
obscuring agricultural subsidies. If returns to the
productive factors provided by the farmer are reasonably
accurate, "pure"[3] subsidies do not accrue to the agricultural sector. Concluding remarks are offered in section four.

INSTITUTIONS, EFFICIENCY MEASURES AND WATER PRICING

In this section attention is focused on changes in
the U.S. institutional framework relevant for assessing
water reclamation projects, as manifested in changing
national objectives for water development, and the implications of these changes for project efficiency measures
and for water pricing policies. As mentioned above, matters related to the consistency of these issues are discussed below in section three.

Multiple purpose planning was not used in assessing
water development projects in the U.S. until the late
1930's. Prior to this time, the institutional framework
relevant for assessing the feasibility of using public
funds to finance such projects[4] was one which reflected
national objectives for encouraging the economic development of arid, western lands. In principle, projects were
assessed within a framework wherein all users of project
water were to repay all project costs expended by the
government. Interest charges were imposed on all users of
project water except farmers, whose allocated project
costs were to be repaid interest-free. Repayment periods

were initially set at 10 years in 1902,[5,6] and extended to
40 years in 1926.[7]

Basic to the institutional framework for assessing
water development projects during this period was the
principle that users of project water, particularly the
irrigated agricultural sector, could and should repay all
allocated project costs. In practice, however, irrigation
users of project water were seemingly able to repay but a
small portion of their costs, the result being a series of
laws forgiving or deferring annual repayments by farmers.[8]

Thus, during the period 1877 to late 1930's, national objectives for the development of western water provided an institutional framework for ex ante assessments
of project feasibility wherein the recuperation of public
funds expended was the overriding criterion. Further,
water pricing was based simply on the cost repayment criterion. The use of this criterion resulted in irrigation
projects found feasible ex ante being found ex post infeasible, and subsequently resulted in substantive changes
in the form of U.S. objectives for water development and
the associated framework for analyzing project feasibility
in 1939.

In 1936-1939, national objectives for water resources
development in the U.S., as expressed in the 1936 Flood
Control Act and the 1939 Reclamation Act, set the stage
for multiple purpose planning as the appropriate institutional framework for assessing water projects. In terms
of project feasibility, the rule was simple: that benefits,
"...to whomsoever they may accrue...",[9] exceed project
costs. Benefits, so defined, were extended to cover any
and all social benefits that might be attributable to a
project.

The range of benefits used for multipurpose planning
for water projects during the 1939-73 period would generally include those given in Table 1 (in addition to electric power generation and municipal-industrial uses). To
provide the reader with some feel for the relative magnitude of these benefit components, average values for each
component drawn from 18 Bureau of Reclamation projects in
the States of Wyoming, Montana, North Dakota and South
Dakota are also included. Viewing data in Table 1 as
descriptive of a composite project in the 1939-73 period,
total benefits of $2,013,000 compare with roughly $635,000
of direct farm benefits which would have been viewed as
benefits under the institutional framework of water planning that existed during the pre-1939 period.

Associated with the change in the institutional
framework for assessing social benefits and costs that
occurred in 1939 was a change in water pricing policies.
Prior to 1939, as noted above, water pricing was based
simply on the notion that users of project water repay
all project costs, with agriculture being forgiven all
interest costs. Two major changes occurred in 1939,

TABLE 6.1

BENEFITS INCLUDED IN BENEFIT-COST STUDIES
FOR MULTIPLE PURPOSE PROJECTS IN THE U.S.

(excluding Power and M & I)

BENEFIT COMPONENT	AVERAGE VALUE FROM 18 PROJECTS
	(thousands of 1979 dollars)
1. Irrigation Benefits	$1,228
Direct Farm Benefits: gross farm income less all production costs.	635
Indirect Farm Benefits: increases in net incomes from farm-related marketing and processing.	461
Public Irrigation Benefits: farm-related increases in incomes from settlement opportunities and employment/investment opportunities.	132
2. Area Redevelopment Benefits: wage payments to unemployed labor from redevelopment areas during project construction and for operation/-maintenance of project irrigation system (off-farm).	486[*]
3. Other Social Benefits: flood control, recreation, environmental-pollution effects and fish/wildlife enhancement.	299

---

[*]Only one of the 18 projects, the Oahe project, included area redevelopment benefits; data given is for the Oahe project.

both of which reflect the changing institutional framework described above. First, paralleling the introduction of social benefits in benefit-cost analyses the
notion of non-reimbursable costs was introduced. Thus,
a portion of project costs -- on the average some 15%[10]
-- is "allocated" to project features in the "Other Social Benefits" category (Table 1) as non-reimbursable
costs. Such costs are borne by the public as a quid-pro-
quo for social or public benefits received. Secondly,
while irrigated agriculture has allocated to it its full
share of project costs, repayment by agriculture is based
on its "ability-to-pay". On the basis of allocated
costs per acre foot of project water diverted for irrigation, irrigation repayment,(based on ability-to-pay)
averaged less than 20% of costs allocated to irrigation.[11]
The difference between allocated costs and irrigation
repayments (based on ability-to-pay) is repaid by excess
power revenues (interest free).[12] Repayment policies for
power and M & I users of project water did not change.
These users repay all allocated project costs plus interest.

Implicit in the above, water pricing remained linked
to the repayment of project costs. Prices were not used
as an allocative mechanism like that described by Howe.[13]
However, in principle, at least, this pricing policy may
be viewed (as in the pre-1939 period) as an effort to use
water charges/prices as a means for society's capture of
resource rents. This particular issue is given more attention below in section three.

Finally, in 1973, still another change in U.S. planning objectives occurred which resulted in a substantial
change in the analytical framework used in assessing net
social benefits attributable to water projects.Pricing
policies were essentially unaffected, however. In 1973
the U.S. Water Resources Council introduced the requirement that benefit-cost measures for water projects be prepared under the assumption that the U.S. economy is fully
employed.[14] The effect of the required full employment
assumption was to exclude from benefit-cost measures those
secondary-induced benefits -- primarily, Indirect and
Public benefits -- that accounted for almost half of irrigation benefits used in the pre-1973 period (Table 1).
The Council's rationale for imposing this assumption is
apparently not based on changes in national objectives
for water developments per se. Nor, it should be noted,
is it based on post-1973 employment conditions: average
unemployment rate for the 13 year period preceeding the
Council's rule was 4.9% compared with average unemployment rates of 6.8% in the post-1973 period (1974-1980).
The full employment assumption was imposed due to weakness
in data and/or measurement methods for assessing secondary
benefits.[15] Thus, the institutional change involved here,
as it relates to changes in frameworks used for assessing

social benefits attributable primarily to irrigation
features of water projects, is a fiat from the Water
Resources Council.

In summary, U.S. objectives vis-a-vis water projects
have essentially moved through three distinct phases, and
changes in these objectives have had profound impacts on
institutional frameworks used for assessing the social
feasibility of expending public funds for water development projects. The first phase might be referred to as
the "market phase" in that, in principle, water resource
development was limited to that which could be supported
-- repaid -- by market returns to water users (primarily
agriculture). Government involvement was limited to providing "up-front" monies which were to be repaid in full,
aside from the interest subsidy to farmers. For planners
in developing countries facing institutional frameworks
similar to that in the U.S. during its market phase, it
must be noted that the market principle broke down in
practice. In the end, the market principle was inconsis-
tent with national goals for water development in the
West, and ex post government involvement in terms of
actual cost bearing was substantial.

The government's role in water resources development
was given explicit form after the late 1930's. Water projects were viewed as serving multiple purpose functions
during the "social phase" in the U.S. between 1939 and
1973. Society-wide benefits associated with flood control, recreation and off-farm economic development were
recognized as public in nature and costs therefore were
to be paid by the public. Water pricing during this
period was based on newly defined resource rents (discussed in section three) far removed from allocative
efficiency criteria. In considering institutional frameworks similar to that extant during the U.S.'s social
phase, planners in developing countries must be drawn to
considerations concerning the potential for generating
public benefits via water development projects and the
formulation of relative priorities in terms of expenditures of scarce public funds.

It is difficult to characterize the post-1973 third
phase in the evolution of institutional frameworks for
water resources developments in the U.S. for several reasons. The restriction of benefits allowed in benefit-cost
measures for assessing the social efficiency of projects
attending the 1973 imposition of the full employment
assumption may be interpreted in any number of ways.[16]
In any case, however, the relevance of this phase for
planners in developing countries must be limited for the
following reasons. By 1973, the bulk of western waters
amenable to reclamation had been developed. 145 Bureau
of Reclamation projects had been authorized with more
than $19 billion (1978 dollars) in authorized construction
expenditures. These projects involved 288 storage dams

and dikes with storage capacities in excess of 135 million
acre feet, 140 diversion dams, 6962 miles of canals, more
than 15 million irrigable acres and 11,700 miles of shore-
line for recreations.[17] Thus, by 1973 one sees the end of
an era in the U.S. wherein broad, national development
objectives might be accomplished through water reclamation projects.   "...Even the casual observer of the
Federal interest in water resources development will have
perceived the end of an era".[18]

WATER PRICING POLICIES, COST ALLOCATIONS AND SUBSIDIES
TO AGRICULTURE

     In the previous section we traced the historical path
of policy objectives throughout the course of U.S. Reclamation history. Initially, it was expected that particularly the agricultural sector would repay the costs of
providing the agricultural features of a project. It be-
came overtly clear, however, that agriculture was generally unable to do this. The repayment criterion was then
displaced by benefit-cost social accounting analyses
wherein questions of project feasibility were distinct from
questions concerning repayment of project costs. It was
then at least implicitly recognized that the goal of U.S.
Reclamation policy was "to create an irrigated empire in
the West".[19] Such considerations are presumably reflec-
tions of the fact that there may be other benefits attending the establishment of a broad based agricultural sector in addition to those associated with net increases in
farm production; e.g., income maintenance, income stabi-
lization, self-dependence, the establishment of modern
day industry etc. These benefits may be particularly important in developing countries. The above considerations
are well-recognized but often difficult to incorporate
into benefit-cost analyses. To the extent this is true,
however, subsidies to the agricultural sector may be appropriate in terms of overall policy objectives.[20]
     If in fact, irrigated agriculture is to be subsi-
dized, it is desirable that the magnitude of such subsidies be readily demonstrable inasmuch as these data may
be important for purposes of global project assessments.
For multipurpose projects, however, problems encountered
in the determination of water pricing policies and in the
allocation of project costs among   project features can
result in distorted measures for subsidies to the agricultural sector. This has been the case in the U.S. as
is made manifest by the ongoing controversy as to the
"actual" subsidy to irrigated agriculture from U.S. water
reclamation projects.[21] An appreciation of these problems
as they have evolved in the assessment of multipurpose
water reclamation projects in the U.S. may then be useful
to planners in developing countries in their efforts to
develop appropriate analytical frameworks for project

assessments wherein subsidies to agriculture may be an
important consideration.

We begin by considering the issue of allocating project costs among the various project "features" (M & I
uses of water, flood control, recreation, irrigation,
etc.) The procedure for allocating costs used by U.S.
agencies is described as follows. The typical structure
for project benefits in a multipurpose project is given
in Table 2. Note, particularly, that net agricultural
benefits includes benefits to others than farmers: indirect and public benefits. At issue is the allocation of
total project costs, C, between n-project features (n=6 in
Table 2) as given in Table 2. Total costs allocated to
feature i are the sum of separable costs, SC_i, and
joint costs, JC_i. Separable costs for feature i are
estimated as the increase in total project costs attributable to i; i.e., SC_i is C less the estimated costs of
a project that would be built without providing for use i
(e.g., storage capacity for flood control or recreation).
Joint costs are project costs in excess of separable costs
which can be attributed to each feature; i.e., total costs
joint costs, JC, equals C less the sum of all SC_i's
$(JC = C - \Sigma JC_i)$.

All else equal, the method used by U.S. agencies to
allocate JC between features would seem to be unobjec-
tionable: they are allocated on the basis of each feature's net contribution to project benefits.[22] (PB_i, net
of SC_i). Thus, defining $X_i = PB_i - SC_i$, joint costs allocated to feature i is determined by

(1)
$$JC_i = \frac{X_i}{\sum\limits_i X_i} \; JC \; ,$$

and total costs allocated to feature i are given by

(2)
$$C_i = SC_i + JC_i$$

Setting aside for the moment issues related to
water pricing/repayment policies discussed below , let
P_t denote periodic water charges paid by irrigated agriculture and r be the social discount rate, and suppose
that:

(3)
$$\sum_{t=1}^{T} P_t(1+r)^{-t} < C_A \quad (i = A \text{ for agriculture}),$$

and

(3')
$$S = C_A - \sum_{t=1}^{T} P_t(1+r)^{-t}$$

TABLE 6.2

TYPICAL STRUCTURE OF PROJECT BENEFITS

AGRICULTURAL BENEFITS

> DIRECT BENEFITS Private: arising from changes in net farm income; presumably to be captured by the farm owner.

> INDIRECT BENEFITS Public: private benefits for which the recipient cannot be identified; arising from additional marketing, transportation, etc., of agricultural products.

> PUBLIC BENEFITS Public: No identifiable recipient; reduced soil erosion, improvements in general welfare, etc.

MUNICIPAL AND INDUSTRIAL BENEFITS

> Private: increased supplies of M & I water; measured by opportunity costs of provision from an alternative source.

RECREATION BENEFITS

> Public: boating, camping, parks, etc.: measured by $$/visitor day x estimated increase in visitor days.

FISH AND WILDLIFE BENEFITS

> Public: fishing and hunting, by type, $$/visitor day x estimated increase in visitor days; enhancement valued at cost.

FLOOD CONTROL BENEFITS

> Public: expected average reduction in agricultural, residential and business flood damages.

POWER BENEFITS

> Private: net value of sales.

OTHER BENEFITS

> Usually public: area redevelopment, externalities, unemployment reduction, etc.

From (3'), the question of interest is: does S appropriately measure the project subsidy to irrigated agriculture? In responding to this question, we begin by noting that two types of costs are defined in U.S. laws related to water reclamation projects: reimbursable costs and non-reimbursable costs. Reimbursable costs are those allocated costs which must be repaid; non-reimbursable costs are costs allocated to features which are social, or public in nature (e.g., flood control and recreation) and, hence, are to be born by society. A curiosity then can be seen in the U.S. practice for allocating project costs to irrigation: included in the measure for agriculture benefits are social benefits -- indirect and public benefits, on the average some 40% of agricultural benefits[23] -- which are recognized neither in the determination of separable costs for agriculture (and its allocation between reimbursable and non-reimbursable costs) nor in the determination of joint costs allocated to irrigation. Agricultural benefits including social benefits are included in the numerator of the weight used to allocate total joint costs to this feature (X_i in equation (1)). As a result, costs allocated to agriculture are overstated and S given in (3') is not an appropriate measure for the subsidy to that feature.

Elimination of this deficiency for joint costs may be accomplished rather easily: direct agricultural benefits (Table 2) are used in the numerator of the weight in equation (1) used to allocate joint costs. The task is more formidable in the case of separable costs inasmuch as one is faced with the following problem: SC_A are separable costs for the irrigation feature which are independent of external social benefits which attend the generation of direct (private) irrigation benefits. The issue as to a "fair share" of SC_A which might be appropriately borne by external beneficiaries of irrigation -- society -- is then an open question.[24]

In addition to these problems associated with accounting practices used in allocating project costs to irrigation, the magnitude of agricultural subsidies is further obscured in U.S. project assessments by water pricing/repayment policies.[25] As noted above in section two, U.S. water pricing policies relevant for agriculture are based on the notion of "ability to pay". Farmers' ability to pay, P_t, is determined in the following manner. First, farm benefits (FB) -- or "direct benefits" as in Table 2 -- are determined via commonly used methods wherein project-related increases in farm production costs are subtracted from increases in gross farm revenues. FB are the direct component of project benefits attributable to irrigation (PB_A) used for benefit-cost assessments of the project. A family "living allowance" is then estimated, as are allowances for such things as risk, which results in an estimation for an amount U_t, where U_t is seemingly a minimum return which must accrue to the farmer if he is to have sufficient incentive to participate in the project. While not given formal treatment in U.S. agency regulations, implicit in the measure U_t is the argument that U_t represents necessary factor payments to the farm family if production is to take place. Ignoring, as we must here, the potential for hidden subsidies in U_t, U_t is a factor payment analogous to the purchase of any other farm input, in which case the irrigation project generates resource rents -- producer surplus in this case[26] -- in the amount $P_t = FB_t - U_t$, and such rents (the farmer's ability to pay) are then captured by society via a water pricing/repayment policy whereby the farmer pays P_t to the treasury.

The implications of this water pricing policy for the determination of subsidies to agriculture are a bit confounding. The use of FB for the purpose of assessing social benefits and costs attributable to the project implies in social accounting terms that social opportunity costs associated with the productive factors earning the return U_t are zero -- those farm resources which earn the return U_t are unemployed resources. In these terms, there is no subsidy to irrigation farmers, ceteris paribus, inasmuch as the use of farmer's resources provide a social quid pro quo for U_t and P_t is returned to the government. As with most (if not all) public projects, distributional questions are involved here inasmuch as farm incomes rise as a result of the employment of their (previously unemployed) resources at the expense of the general public,[27] but a subsidy per se cannot be charged to agriculture so long as U_t accurately reflects the farmer's preferences between the use and non-use of productive factors (loosely, his work-leisure preferences at the margin).[28]

From the above we may draw some conclusions, continuing to assume that U_t is an appropriate measure of returns to the input of productive factors by the farmer. First, if such factors are fully employed prior to the initiation of the project, subsidies clearly do not accrue to agriculture: all resource rents, $P_t = FB_t - U_t$, accrue to the public. It follows, however, that FB should not be used in the project's benefit-cost measure. The appropriate measure for direct, net social benefits attributable to the irrigation feature is P_t in this case. When such factors are unemployed without the project, FB is an appropriate measure for net social benefits attributable to irrigation and pure subsidies do not accrue to farmers. Ceteris paribus, pure subsidies obtain only in the case where U_t is found to be in excess of fair market returns (on surrogates therefor) to farm inputs underlying the return U_t.

CONCLUDING REMARKS

Planners in developing countries may find interesting the history of U.S. reclamation policy given the extremes reflected by these policies between the pre-1939 "market" phase and the post-1939 "social" phase. Of particular interest should be the operational failure of the pre-1939 market phase wherein principle and practice were widely divergent. Of further interest to these planners may be water pricing and cost allocation practices followed in the U.S. as they relate to agricultural subsidies. One finds in the U.S. experience methodological practices which have had the effect of obscuring the level of subsidies to irrigated agriculture. Planners in developing countries may wish to reflect on these issues in their efforts to promulgate assessment practices relevant for their institutional setting. In conjunction with Howe's discussions concerning principles relevant for the assessment of multi-purpose water projects, it is hoped that this discussion of the U.S. experience will be useful to the planner in these efforts.

Footnotes

1. Charles W. Howe,   "Socially Efficient Development and Allocation of Water in Developing Countries: Roles for the Public and Private Sectors."

2. Ibid., Section IV.B.

3. As used here, pure subsidies refer to financial transfers between the government and farmers; i.e., farmers receive monies without exchanging services worth a corresponding value.

4. Multiple purpose planning was formally recognized in the Flood Control Act of 1936 (Act of June 22, 1936, Ch. 688, 49 Stat. 1570) and established as a basis for assessing BuRec projects in Reclamation Project Act of 1939 (Act of August 4, 1939, Ch. 418, 54 Stat. 1187). Congressional appropriations for water projects did not begin until 1915; see H. S. Burness, R. G. Cummings, W. D. Gorman and R. R. Lansford, "United States Reclamation Policy and Indian Water Rights", Natural Resource Journal, Vol. 20, October 1980, pp. 807-826.

5. Reclamation Act of June 17, 1902, Ch. 1093, 32 Stat. 388.

6. Act of August 13, 1914, Ch. 247, 38 Stat. 686.

7. Omnibus Adjustment Act of May 25, 1926, Ch. 383, 44 Stat. 636.

8. Burness, et al., Op. Cit., pp. 809-811.

9. Ibid., pp. 812-813.

10. Ibid., p. 822.

11. Ibid., p. 821

12. For a discussion of "excess power revenues: and the related "Basin Accounts", see Burness, et. al, Op. Cit., pp. 821-822.

13. Op. Cit., Section IV.B.

14. 38 Federal Register, 24,777 (1973), see, also, final rules given in 45 Federal Register, September, 1980.

15. 45 Federal Register, Op. Cit., p. 64372.

16. Throughout these earlier discussions we have abstracted from criticisms regarding BuRec practices in preparing benefit-cost analyses as well as questions concerning the logic underlying measures for secondary benefits; in this latter regard, see H. H. Stoevener and R. G. Kraynick, "On Augmenting Community Economic Performance by New or Continuing Irrigation Developments", American Journal of Agricultural Economics., December 1979.

17. U.S. Department of the Interior, BuRec, "Water and Land Resource Accomplishments - Appendix 2", Washington, D.C., 1973, p. i.

18. Stoevener, H. H. and R. G. Kraynick, Op. Cit., p. 1122.

19. See 51 Congressional Record 13,453 (1915), (Remarks of Representative Hayden).

20. Clearly, subsidies have historically been more closely related to political interests in many cases. However, this is just a realization of the fact that economic data are just one input into a decision process.

21. For example, see D. Seckler and R. A. Young, "Economic and Policy Implications of the 160-Acre Limitations in Federal Reclamation Law", American Journal of Agricultural Economics, Vol. 60, No. 4, November, 1978, pp. 565-600; also, see R. A. Young, "Economic Analysis and Federal Irrigation Policy", Western Agricultural Economic Journal, December, 1978, pp. 257-267.

22. In fact, JC is allocated on the basis of relative "alternative costs" or benefits (see Burness, et al., Op. Cit., Section III); net benefits are used here for expository purposes, particularly for irrigation, inasmuch as benefits are the criteria most often used.

23. Ibid.

24. A method which is at least consistent with other allocative procedures described above would be the assignment of the proportion [Direct Agricultural Benefits ÷ Total Agricultural Benefits] of SC_A to the irrigation feature.

25. In what follows we ignore "repayment" of those costs allocated to irrigation which are charged to Basin Accounts given that, in the end, such "repayments" are simply transfers; see Burness, et. al., Op. Cit.

26. With the usual price-taker assumption wherein prices for project-related outputs are assumed unaffected by the increase in production, increases in consumer surplus do not obtain.

27. Assuming, as is generally the case, that the present value of the payment P_t is less that project costs which are appropriately allocated to irrigation.

28. We acknowledge the potential for inconsistencies in this argument. Strictly speaking, U_t as defined here may be viewed as the farmers' reservation price for productive factors under his control, in which case the discription "unemployed" becomes meaningless in social accounting terms, U_t measures a non-zero opportunity cost and, therefore, should be subtracted from FB in the benefit-cost measure. This conclusion is weakened, however, by another practice by BuRec wherein FB used for determining ability to pay is less than direct farm benefits (see, e.g., Dolores Project Colorado Definite Plan Report, U.S. BuRec, April, 1977); this difference is attributable to the fact that price inflation is included in the latter measure but not in the former. Thus, any inflation in farm prices reduces the real value of rents paid thereby constituting a form of a subsidy.

Index

148

Lifestyles
and fishery management, 26
Limited entry programs
(fishing), 17-22
license transferal, 18, 25
monopolies and, 25
small fishermen and, 25-26
Lumber, 37, 41, 43. See also
Wood products

Maintenance research. See
Agricultural research,
maintenance
Marine resources. See Fisheries
and fisheries management
Market interdependency. See
Water and water management,
interdependencies
Maximum sustained yield (MSY),
11
Metals. See Non-renewable
resources
Mexico
agricultural research in, 75
water management in, 124,
125, 126(Table 5.3)
MSY. See Maximum sustained
yield

New Zealand
forest plantations in, 53
Non-renewable resources, 1
North America
agricultural productivity
in, 70
agricultural research in,
65, 67, 73, 78, 80(Table 4.2),
81, 83, 84-85, 92(n4)
fishing regulations in,
13-14, 21
forestry in, 42-43, 45, 54,
55(Table 3.6)
labor productivity in, 71,
92(n7)
water management in, 96
(Figure 5.1), 100(Table 5.1),
109, 111, 124, 128-129(n10),
130-136

Northern Colorado Water Conservancy
District, 120, 129(n11)

Open access, 9-10, 98
to water, 101-102
See also Limited entry programs
Ores. See Non-renewable resources
"Organization of Research to Improve
Crops and Animals in Low-income
Countries," 82-83
Otsuka, Keijiro, 88-89

Peru
labor productivity in, 71
Philippines
labor productivity in, 71
Plantations. See Forest plantations
Pollutants
in water, 97-98
Priority rights systems. See Water
and water management, rights
systems
Productivity
agricultural, 69-71, 78, 89
labor, 70-71, 92(n7)
Property rights, 4
and fishing, 6
water, 101-102, 108-119
See also Open access
Proportionate rights systems. See
Water and water management, rights
systems

Quality interdependencies. See
Water and water management, interdependencies
Quotas (fishing)
individual, 22-24
overall, 13, 28
small fishermen and, 25-26
transfer of, 23
See also Data

Recreation, 36
Regulations. See Intervention;
individual resources
Research
adaptive, 3, 73-74, 89-90
agricultural. See Agricultural
research
basic vs applied, 65-67